# THE NEW PORTLAND, MAINE CHEF'S TABLE

## EXTRAORDINARY RECIPES FROM THE COAST OF MAINE

MARGARET HATHAWAY

PHOTOGRAPHS BY KARL SCHATZ

Down East Books

Camden, Maine

# Down East Books

Published by Down East Books
An imprint of Globe Pequot
Trade division of The Rowman & Littlefield Publishing Group, Inc.
4501 Forbes Blvd., Ste. 200
Lanham, MD 20706
www.rowman.com
www.downeastbooks.com
Distributed by NATIONAL BOOK NETWORK

British Library Cataloguing in Publication Information available

**Library of Congress Cataloging-in-Publication Data**

Names: Hathaway, Margaret, author. | Schatz, Karl, photographer.
Title: The new Portland, Maine chef's table : extraordinary recipes from
the coast of Maine / Margaret Hathaway ; photographs by Karl Schatz.
Description: Lanham, MD : Down East Books
An imprint of Globe Pequot, 2019. | Includes index.
Identifiers: LCCN 2019002599 (print) | LCCN 2019004093 (ebook) | ISBN
9781608939893 (Electronic) | ISBN 9781608939596 (cloth : alk. paper)
Subjects: LCSH: Cooking—Maine—Portland. | LCGFT: Cookbooks.
Classification: LCC TX715 (ebook) | LCC TX715 .H364 2019 (print) |
DDC 641.59741/91—dc23
LC record available at https://lccn.loc.gov/2019002599

♾™ The paper used in this publication meets the minimum requirements
of American National Standard for Information Sciences—Permanence of
Paper for Printed Library Materials, ANSI/NISO Z39.48-1992.

Printed in the United States of America.

*To Charlotte, Beatrice, and Sadie Schatz—great eaters all!*
*There's something in here for each of you.*

# CONTENTS

## Dutch's | 51

Wild Maine Blueberry Muffins 52

Popovers Benedict 53

## Eaux | 57

Red Beans and Rice 58

Drop Biscuits and Andouille Gravy 59

Bananas Foster 60

## Forage | 63

Cranberry Bran Muffins 65

7-Grain Bread 66

## High Roller Lobster | 69

Lobster Grilled Cheese 69

Lobster Bisque 70

## Izakaya Minato | 73

Dashi 74

Hot Soba Broth 74

Cold Soba Dipping Broth 74

*Shiromi Ankake*
(Whitefish Topped with Sauce) 75

## LB Kitchen | 77

Avocado Addiction 79

Tofu Banh Mi Bowl 79

## Little Giant | 83

Cabbage with Whipped Halibut
and Celery Root Puree 84

Brussels Sprouts with Mojo Picon
and Blue Cheese Sauce 87

Beef Tenderloin with Uni Butter, Matsutake
Mushrooms, Littleneck Clams,
and Smoked Spruce 89

## Liquid Riot 93

Mushroom Toast 94

Fernet Michaud Ice Cream 95

"I Only Drink Beer" Cocktail 96

## Salvage Barbecue | 155
Evil Death Slather #6 (Blueberry Hot Sauce) 156

Cornbread Muffins 156

## Scales | 161
Kohlrabi Salad 162

Baked Haddock with Fumet Sauce 164

## Solo Italiano | 167
Lobster and Borage Lasagna 169

## Sur Lie | 173
Rossejat 174

Russian Potato Salad with Trout Roe
and Piquillo Emulsion 177

Lemon Curd with Graham Crackers
and Swiss Meringue 178

## Ten Ten Pié | 181
Pistachio Olive Oil Cake 182

Coconut Milk Panna Cotta 183

## Terlingua | 187
Pork Green Chili 189

*Enchiladas Suizas* (Potato Enchiladas) 191

## The Shop at Island Creek Oysters | 193
Champagne Mignonette 194

Grilled Oysters with Herbed Bottarga Butter
and Preserved Lemon 194

## Tin Pan Bakery | 197
Blueberry Cornmeal Bars 198

Rhubarb Crumb Cake 199

## Tipo | 203
Spicy Pork Ragu with Oregano
and Mascarpone 204

Caramelized Onion Focaccia 205

# INTRODUCTION

Take a stroll along any street in Portland, and chances are, you'll be tempted by one of the city's extraordinary eateries. Stretched along the shores of picturesque Casco Bay, the city of Portland boasts an astonishing concentration of great restaurants and a food community with a sense of camaraderie and purpose. On the city's main peninsula—which reaches from the Munjoy Hill neighborhood and its Eastern Promenade at one side, to the West End, edged by the mouth of the Fore River, at the other—sit nearly one hundred restaurants, spanning a great diversity of flavors, enthusiasms, and price points. Expand your search to the city limits, and you'll find more than four hundred.

Since the publication of the first *Portland, Maine, Chef's Table* cookbook in 2012, the city has continued its culinary transformation. While its many tourists once associated the flavors of Portland with the lobster and chowder spots that jut out on wharfs over the working waterfront, in the past decade there's been a renaissance that's resulted in a wide array of cuisines. Wafting over the city are the mingled scents of buttery French pastry, pungent Vietnamese noodles, Japanese *izakaya*-style street foods, wood-fired Milanese pizza, slow-cooked barbecue, Middle Eastern *mezze*, and more. The city that was named "Foodiest Small Town in America" by *Bon Appetit* magazine in 2009 was upgraded to "Restaurant City of the Year" in 2018.

There are many reasons for this profusion of flavors. Portland's geographical situation—water on both sides and close proximity to the farms of southern Maine—gives chefs access to a great variety of local ingredients, from grass-fed beef to farmstead cheeses to the daily catch coming in

on countless fishing boats. The area's farm-to-table movement began decades ago, urged on by the Maine Organic Farmers and Gardeners Association, the first organization of its kind in the country, and a group that many Portland chefs are proud to support. This connection between growers and chefs has encouraged the cultivation (and, in some cases, resurrection) of heirloom ingredients—don't be surprised to find salsify, burdock root, husk cherries, and Tolman Sweet apples on menus around town. Lately some chefs have taken it a step further, growing and raising their own produce, livestock, and honeybees. The access and commitment to using local ingredients, in a region with such harsh winters and short growing seasons, has also led chefs to experiment with methods of food preservation. House-made pickles, preserves, and charcuterie are found on menus throughout Portland, and cocktails are crafted with simple syrups and bitters infused with local herbs.

Beyond ingredients, the city of Portland itself has shaped its vibrant cuisine. Rich in history, reaching back beyond the first European settlement in 1633 to the Abenaki Native Americans who originally lived on the peninsula, Portland has been subject to regular periods of reinvention, brought on centuries ago by four devastating fires, and more recently by a combination of immigration and urban renewal. The city's motto, *Resurgam*, Latin for "I will rise again," and the phoenix depicted on its seal, reference a series of fires that destroyed the town in its first centuries. The historic Old Port, with its cobbled streets and charming brick buildings, was built after the most recent fire, on Independence Day of 1866. Around that time, construction flourished throughout the peninsula, giving Portland Deering Oaks Park, a narrow gauge railway, and an abundance of stately, architecturally significant homes. Though subject to sprawl and suburban expansion over the next hundred years, the last two decades of the twentieth century brought revitalization to downtown Portland: Residential neighborhoods like Munjoy Hill and the West End experienced dramatic gentrification, the Arts District on Congress Street saw the construction of a new building complex for the Portland Museum of Art by the firm of I. M. Pei, and the Old Port was transformed into the area of boutiques and restaurants it is today.

The period also saw an influx of immigrants from near and far: A growing African population came to escape oppressive conditions in their homelands, while Americans from urban centers came to Portland searching for Maine's state motto, "The way life should be." Many in the culinary community have migrated north from New York and Boston, or returned home to open restaurants in their native Maine. Drawn by a feeling of camaraderie and healthy balance, chefs have found room to explore and experiment, opening food carts and trucks, working in collaborative spaces, and supporting each other and their purveyors. A great number of Portland's restaurants are run by couples, a shift reflected in the rise of breakfast and lunch spots (see Dutch's, LB Kitchen, and Rose Foods), and family-friendly eateries with kids' menus and easy parking (see Woodford Food & Beverage and Tipo).

Despite its small size—fewer than seventy thousand inhabitants in the city proper—Portland balances a thriving cultural life with a commitment to ecological conservation. The city supports a symphony and ballet company, a world-class art museum, and, of course, its vivid culinary scene, while also living up to its former nickname, The Forest City, dotting the town with green spaces that include pockets of woods, the Fore River Sanctuary, and Portland Trails, a system of connected walking trails. With a population of such diverse interests, it's fitting that Portland would have an equally varied food scene.

This book is an invitation to explore Portland through its unique flavors, and through Karl's beautiful photographs of the city. When making the recipes, we hope you'll keep a few things in mind:

· While we've tried to scale all the dishes to serve six to eight people, some, particularly sauces, are made for a crowd. Most pickles and sauces will keep in the refrigerator for up to two weeks. Extras can also be placed in sterilized mason jars for a lovely gift.
· At the opposite end of the spectrum, some sandwiches and cocktails in the book are meant to be assembled individually, and make a single serving. Simply multiply if you're making more.
· For breads and pastas, most chefs weigh their ingredients to keep the proportions standard. We have converted the ingredients to cups and teaspoons, but we've left the chefs' metric weights in parenthesis. If you have a kitchen scale, try weighing your ingredients.
· Most recipes can be made in any well-equipped kitchen. If special equipment is required, it will be mentioned in the headnote.
· As with any recipe, feel free to adjust seasonings and ingredients to taste.

If you've visited Portland, perhaps you'll find the recipe for an amazing dish you tasted. If you haven't yet made it to Casco Bay, we hope this book will inspire you to take a trip north.

BRUNCH
DINNER
DESSERT
BEER
WINE
COCKTAILS

# BAHARAT

91 Anderson Street
(207) 613-9849
*baharatmaine.com*
Chef/Owner: Clayton Norris
Co-Owner: Jenna Friedman

This warm and welcoming corner cafe brings Middle Eastern street foods to the up-and-coming East Bayside neighborhood. Hung with elaborate punched tin lights, busy geometric patterns, and walls of garage door–style windows that open in summer, Baharat is the brick-and-mortar incarnation of Chef Clayton Norris and Jenna Friedman's popular CN Shawarma food truck. Now patrons can sip intricate cocktails at the zinc bar while they snack on fried cauliflower and house-made pickles, but the menu is still stacked with food truck favorites like the Shawarmageddon, "a plus-size sandwich stuffed with chicken, falafel, house fries, and all the sauces."

While working at a French restaurant early in his career, Maine native Chef Norris was introduced to the flavors of the Middle East by an Egyptian coworker, and since then he's been hooked. Named for a traditional spice blend (*baharat* means "spice" in Arabic), the restaurant roots this palate in Maine's bounty, incorporating local produce and regional touches into its offerings. The menu is a combination of skewered and grilled meats, deconstructed riffs on classics like tabbouleh (served here with a seasonal sunchoke cream),
vegetarian main dishes of hearty vegetables and grains, and generous bowls of garlicky sauces. The Turkish crab dip caught the attention of *Bon Appetit*'s editors and earned the restaurant a mention in the magazine's 2018 feature on Portland.

One of the most popular items on the food truck's menu, the Chicken Shawarma Kabob, has stayed a house favorite. On the truck they would stack eighty pounds of butterflied chicken thighs on a vertical spit and shave it into sandwiches. At the restaurant they use the same marinade and cut of meat, but thread it on stainless-steel skewers and grill it over an open flame.

While it does take some planning ahead, fresh hummus is such an improvement over store-bought varieties that it's worth the effort. When served straight from the food processor, drizzled generously with tahini and olive oil, it is almost unrecognizable to its supermarket cousin.

Muhammara is a Syrian spread that is quickly gaining popularity, for good reason. It's earthy, sweet, tart, and satisfying. Serve it alone with pita, or on the side of grilled meats, like the Chicken Shawarma Kabob featured here.

# CHICKEN SHAWARMA KABOB

## (MAKES 12 10-INCH SKEWERS)

10 pounds boneless, skinless chicken thighs

Marinade

Knob of ginger (approximately 2 x 1 inch)

8 cloves garlic

2 tablespoons kosher salt

1 cup full-fat Greek yogurt

½ cup extra virgin olive oil

½ cup apple cider vinegar

2 lemons

1 orange

½ teaspoon ground cloves

2 teaspoons ground allspice

½ teaspoon cardamom

1 teaspoon cinnamon

1 tablespoon smoked hot paprika

1 tablespoon turmeric

2 tablespoons coriander

2 tablespoons dried mint

1 teaspoon cayenne pepper

2 teaspoons sumac

1 tablespoon cumin

**To prepare the chicken:** Rinse chicken pieces and pat dry with paper towels. Remove any remaining sinew or large pieces of fat from each piece of chicken. Cut each thigh into four or five even pieces, depending on the size of the piece. Place chicken pieces into a large bowl and set aside in the refrigerator while you make the marinade.

**To prepare the marinade:** Peel the ginger and garlic cloves. Place in the bowl of a food processor with the kosher salt. Puree the ingredients until they become a paste, scraping down the sides of the bowl as needed. Add the yogurt, olive oil, and vinegar to the paste. Blend in the processor until fully incorporated.

Place the blended ingredients in a large bowl. Zest 1 lemon and half of the orange into the bowl. Squeeze the lemon and the orange, and add the juice to the bowl. Add all the dried spices and whisk until all ingredients are fully incorporated.

Pour the marinade over the prepared chicken and mix to fully cover all the pieces. Set aside in the refrigerator for 2 to 4 hours.

**To grill the chicken:** Preheat grill on medium heat. When ready to grill, assemble your skewers. Slide the individual pieces of chicken onto each skewer, providing each one with roughly the same amount of chicken. Place skewers on the grill to cook for 8 to 10 minutes. Turn once, taking care to allow for the proper amount of caramelization on the meat. Serve with pita bread, hummus, muhammara, and your favorite pickled vegetables.

# HUMMUS

(MAKES 6-8 SERVINGS)

2½ cups dried chickpeas

2 tablespoons kosher salt

7 cloves garlic

1 cup tahini

Juice of 2–3 lemons

6 tablespoons cold water

½ cup olive oil, plus more for serving

Chopped fresh parsley, for garnish

Place chickpeas in a large pot and add enough water that they're covered by 3 to 4 inches. Soak overnight.

The following day, drain the chickpeas and place in a saucepan large enough to hold the chickpeas and 4 quarts of water. Bring to a simmer over medium-high heat. Cook chickpeas at a simmer for at least 2 hours, skimming the foam as it rises to the top. The chickpeas are done when they barely hold their shape and are completely soft and creamy.

Drain the cooked chickpeas and place in the bowl of a food processor. Blend until broken down and completely smooth. Add remaining ingredients (except parsley) and blend until completely incorporated. The longer you blend the hummus, the smoother it will be.

Serve with a generous sprinkle of parsley, a drizzle of olive oil, and warm flatbread for dipping.

# MUHAMMARA

(MAKES 6-8 SERVINGS)

8 red bell peppers

½ cup torn pita bread

½ cup walnuts

2 shallots

3 cloves garlic

4 tablespoons olive oil

Juice of 1 lemon

1 tablespoon sherry vinegar

1 tablespoon pomegranate molasses

1 tablespoon kosher salt

Pomegranate seeds, for garnish

Toasted walnut halves, for garnish

Roast the red peppers over an open flame until they are evenly charred and the flesh starts to soften. This can be done over the flame on a gas stove or grill, or under a broiler. If using a broiler, make sure to turn the peppers periodically to ensure even roasting.

Meanwhile, preheat the oven to 350°F. Place the pita bread and walnuts on a rimmed baking sheet and toast until golden brown and fragrant. Set both aside to cool.

Roughly chop the shallots and garlic. In a small skillet over medium heat, lightly sauté shallots and garlic in 1 tablespoon of olive oil until translucent. Set aside.

Once the peppers are cool enough to handle, remove the charred skins and open each pepper to expose the seeds and ribs. With the back of a paring knife, carefully scrape out the seeds and ribs and remove the stem, leaving only the softened flesh.

Place the toasted pita bread and walnuts in the bowl of a food processor and pulse four or five times to break them down. Add roasted peppers, sautéed shallots and garlic, and all remaining ingredients (except garnishes) to the food processor and blend until the mixture is the consistency of a relish. Serve muhammara at room temperature with warm flatbread, garnished with additional toasted walnuts and pomegranate seeds.

# BELLEVILLE

**1 North Street**
*(207) 536-7463*
*blvl.me*
Chef/Owner: Christopher Deutsch
Co-Owner: Amy Fuller

From a sunlit corner high on Congress Street, the comforting smells of butter and yeast waft through Munjoy Hill. Belleville, a bakery specializing in classic French breakfast and lunch treats, has been delighting the neighborhood since it was opened by husband-and-wife team Chris Deutsch and Amy Fuller in the fall of 2017.

In the bakery's compact kitchen, visible to diners through a high window behind the counter, baker Chris Deutsch draws on his European upbringing and almost a decade of training in both the United States and Paris to create perfectly lacquered croissants, richly caramelized kouign-amann, and morning buns dotted with plump raisins. As the hours pass, a changing array of savory pizzas fill the case. Since it received national attention from *Bon Appetit* magazine in the summer of 2018, Belleville has been discovered by visitors from outside the neighborhood, and summer weekend mornings bring lines out the door. By early afternoon, the pace slows a little, and it's possible to snag a perch on one of the high stools at the street-facing counter, pick yourself up with a cup of coffee and a *pain au chocolat*, and watch the world go by.

Deutsch notes that for all their fanfare, almond croissants are a treat rooted in bakers' thrift: Day-old pastries are split in half, filled with creamy frangipane, topped with a sprinkling of sliced almonds, and rebaked to a toasty crunch. Starting with good croissants is the key to a perfect outcome, as is a lavish, messy-to-eat dusting of confectioners' sugar.

9

# ALMOND CROISSANTS

## (MAKES 6 CROISSANTS)

6 day-old croissants

Simple Syrup (see recipe below)

Frangipane (see recipe below)

Sliced almonds

Confectioners' sugar, for dusting

### Simple Syrup

½ cup granulated sugar

½ cup water

**To make the simple syrup:** Combine sugar and water in a small saucepan and bring to a boil. Remove from heat and let cool. Simple syrup can be stored, covered, in a refrigerator for up to 3 days.

### Frangipane

⅔ cup unsalted butter, softened

¾ cup granulated sugar

3 large eggs, at room temperature

1½ cups almond flour

**To make the frangipane:** Beat butter and sugar in a stand mixer until thoroughly combined. Add eggs, one at a time, and beat until well incorporated. Scrape down the sides of the bowl to ensure that all ingredients are blended. Add almond flour and beat again until thoroughly incorporated. Frangipane can be stored, covered, in a refrigerator for up to 3 days.

**To assemble the almond croissants:** Preheat oven to 400°F. Slice each day-old croissant in half horizontally. Brush interior sides with the simple syrup. On the bottom half of each croissant, spread 2 tablespoons of the frangipane, smoothing to ensure an even layer. Replace the top half of each croissant, and spoon 3 heaping tablespoons of frangipane on the top of each. Sprinkle with sliced almonds. Place assembled croissants on a parchment-lined baking sheet and bake in a preheated oven for approximately 18 minutes, until they are fragrant and lightly toasted. Let cool on the baking sheet and sprinkle generously with confectioners' sugar before serving.

# BLACK COW

83 Exchange Street
(207) 772-7774
*blackcowburgers.com*
Owner: Jay Villani
Chef: Nicholas Nappi
Bar Manager: Mark Hibbard

The latest offering from Chef Jay Villani, owner of the West End mainstay Local 188 and Salvage Barbecue (see page 155), is a family-friendly burger spot in the heart of the Old Port. Located on the spacious ground floor of a landmark building that previously housed Villani's upscale restaurant and bar, Sonny's, Black Cow puts its own spin on an American classic. Billing itself as a "cocktail bar, soda fountain, and burger joint that focuses on handmade food and doubles down on hospitality," Black Cow offers a quintessential mix of all-American favorites, taken to a new level: A cup of tomato soup comes with smoked ricotta, potato fries can be swapped for fried Brussels sprouts, and soda options include house-made hibiscus coconut and ginger lemongrass (see recipe). Burgers are cooked on the griddle and topped with iceberg lettuce and American cheese, but you can make yours veggie with a mushroom and lentil patty topped with black garlic mayonnaise. Milkshakes, egg creams, and sundaes are plentiful, as are a variety of creative cocktails.

Despite its humble name, the Black Cow Burger is complex and carefully constructed. Each strata of the burger is made in house, from the potato roll bun to the smoky mustard to the "special sauce" of caramelized tomato mayo. To be truly authentic to the restaurant version, grind your own brisket for the meat patty, according to the instructions below. Each component of the burger is listed below, in order from longest prep time to shortest. For ingredients that the restaurant kitchen measures by weight, that number is listed in parenthesis. If you don't have time to make them all, Chef Nappi notes that any one of these pieces will enhance your home burger.

For the Black Cow Ginger Lemongrass Soda base, citric acid, also called "sour salt," and arabic powder, also called "gum arabic," are available in the spice section of specialty markets, and online. To make the soda base, you will make two separate batches of syrup and combine them in a 1:1 ratio. Any leftover can be reserved for use in cocktails or other sodas.

---

## BLACK COW BURGER WITH SMOKY MUSTARD, QUICK PICKLES, AND CARAMELIZED TOMATO MAYONNAISE

### (MAKES 1 SERVING)

Potato Roll Bun (see recipe below)

Butter or beef tallow, melted

Smoky Mustard (see recipe below)

Caramelized Tomato Mayonnaise (see recipe below)

Iceberg lettuce, finely shredded

Garlic Dill Quick Pickles (see recipe below)

White onion, thinly shaved into rings and shocked in ice water

Burger patty (grinding instructions below)

American cheese, sliced

## Potato Roll Bun

(MAKES 1 DOZEN BUNS)

1¼ cups (290 grams) milk

¼ cup (50 grams) sugar

2¼ teaspoons (7 grams) dry active yeast

3 cups plus 2 tablespoons (426 grams)
    all-purpose flour

2 tablespoons (23 grams) potato flour

1½ teaspoons (8 grams) salt

⅓ cup (75 grams) butter

2 whole eggs, beaten

Sesame seeds

In a small saucepan over low heat, warm the milk to 110 degrees. Pour warm milk into the bowl of a stand mixer fitted with the dough hook attachment, and sprinkle sugar and yeast over the surface. Turn the mixer on low and let turn a few times to disperse the sugar and yeast.

In a separate medium-size bowl, whisk together flour, potato flour, and salt. With the mixer on low, slowly add the dry ingredients to the milk mixture. Add the butter all at once, and increase the mixer speed to medium-high, kneading until a shiny, cohesive ball is formed. Cover dough and let rest in the refrigerator for 20–30 minutes.

Using a bench scraper, cut dough into lumps that are roughly the size of a golf ball (at the restaurant, they measure 69 grams). Using the palm of your hand, roll dough in a circular motion on a lightly floured workspace, forming a tight ball. Line a baking sheet with parchment paper, and place dough balls on the parchment, leaving enough room between them for the dough to expand. Brush with beaten eggs, and sprinkle with sesame seeds. Gently cover with plastic film, and allow to rise at room temperature until the buns have expanded by double and a quarter. While dough is rising, preheat oven to 350 degrees.

Bake for 10 minutes, then rotate and bake for an additional 5 minutes, checking for doneness. Buns are ready when they're lightly browned but still tender. Once buns are done, let cool to room temperature before assembling burgers.

## Smoky Mustard

(MAKES 2 CUPS)

1¾ plus 2 tablespoons (440 grams) water

¼ cup (50 grams) apple cider vinegar, plus more
    to taste

2 cups (200 grams) ground yellow mustard seeds

1 tablespoon (10 grams) ground turmeric

1 scant teaspoon (3 grams) onion powder

Heaping ½ teaspoon (2 grams) garlic powder

¼ teaspoon (1 gram) smoked paprika

2 cups simple syrup

Salt, to taste

In a large, heavy-bottomed pot over medium heat, combine water and apple cider vinegar. Stir in spices and a pinch of salt. Bring to a simmer and cook, stirring continuously. Reduce the mixture until it has thickened to the consistency of a thick paste. Remove from heat and transfer mixture to a nonreactive container. Cool to room temperature, and put the mixture in the refrigerator for at least one week (preferably two) to cure.

Once the mustard base has cured, continue with the recipe. Working in small batches, place the mustard mixture in a blender, and blend the mustard base with simple syrup and apple cider vinegar, to taste. This will loosen the mixture, while balancing the sweetness and acidity. Salt to taste, then cover tightly and transfer to a nonreactive container to store, refrigerated, for up to two weeks.

## Garlic Dill Quick Pickles

(MAKES 1 GALLON)

| | |
|---|---|
| 4 quarts pickling cucumber, thinly sliced | ½ cup salt |
| 6 cups apple cider vinegar | 20 medium sprigs of dill |
| 3 cups water | 6 garlic cloves, crushed |

Place the cucumber slices in a large, nonreactive, heat-proof container. Combine all other ingredients in a large, heavy-bottomed pot and place over medium-high heat. Once the brine has come to a boil, pour contents over the cucumber slices and cover with a piece of parchment paper to ensure that all the pickles are submerged. Cool to room temperature, cover, and refrigerate for up to 1 week.

## Caramelized Tomato Mayonnaise

(MAKES 4 CUPS)

| | |
|---|---|
| ¼ cup tomato paste | Apple cider vinegar, to taste |
| 2 egg yolks | Salt, to taste |
| 1 whole egg | Ice cubes |
| 1 quart canola oil | |

In a small pan over low heat, cook the tomato paste, stirring frequently until it has thickened and become a light brown color. Set aside paste to cool.

In the bowl of a food processor, combine egg yolk and whole eggs along with a pinch of salt. Run the machine, adding oil in a thin stream to emulsify the mayonnaise. Once the tomato paste has cooled, blend that in as well. Add salt and vinegar to taste, and lastly add a few ice cubes to both thin the condiment slightly and give it a nice sheen.

## The Meat

At Black Cow, beef patties are made from 100% brisket, carefully trimmed and ground. The instructions below will give you the perfect Black Cow Burger, but you can substitute any beef patty, as long as the meat is fresh.

**Grinding instructions for the perfect burger:** Separate the fatty side of the brisket from the lean, following the natural seam of the meat. Trim all the silver skin and fat from the lean side, discarding the silver skin but reserving the fat. Cut the lean meat into strips following the grain of the muscle. Weigh the meat. Calculate 30 percent of the lean meat and weigh out that amount of the reserved fat. Cut the fat into 1-inch-sized chunks. Run lean and fatty meat through a meat grinder on a small-sized die, alternating between the lean meat and the fat. Change to a medium-sized die and run the ground mixture through again, along with the reserved chunks of the fatty side of the brisket.

## The Burger

**To assemble the burger:** For each burger, split a potato roll bun in half and brush both sides with melted butter or beef tallow. Heat a griddle, and place each half of the bun face down on the surface, pressing slightly to ensure even toasting. Weigh four ounces of ground beef, and form the meat into a ball. Place it on the hot griddle, and using a sturdy spatula, press on the meat until it spreads to a thin patty, and sticks to the dry cooking surface. Salt meat liberally. Remove the toasted bun from the griddle, and place open on a plate. Spread Smoky Mustard on the top bun, and Caramelized Tomato Mayonnaise on the bottom bun. Place a bed of iceberg lettuce on the bottom bun, and sliced pickles and onions on the top. On the griddle, flip the burger and immediately top with cheese. When cheese has melted, place the patty on the bottom bun and cover with the top bun. Serve immediately.

# GINGER LEMONGRASS SODA

## (MAKES 1 QUART)

4 cups (200 grams) peeled and chopped fresh ginger

1¾ cups plus 2 tablespoons (200 grams) granulated sugar

¾ cups plus 1 tablespoon (200 grams) water

3⅓ cups (225 grams) lemongrass stalks

1 tablespoon (8 grams) cardamom pods, cracked

4¼ cups (1 liter) water

Scant 3 cups (600 grams) granulated sugar

1 tablespoon (15 grams) citric acid

Scant 1 tablespoon (14 grams) arabic powder

Chop the ginger into small pieces and place in a blender with sugar and water. Blend until sugar is dissolved and ginger is fully pureed. Pour mixture into a nonreactive container, cover, and let stand at room temperature for one hour.

When ginger mixture has steeped, strain through a fine colander or metal chinois. Make sure to press solids thoroughly with a rubber spatula to ensure that the most flavorful syrup is extracted.

On a clean surface, pound the lemongrass stalks with a kitchen mallet, then slice into small pieces. In a medium-size saucepan, place the chopped lemongrass and cardamom pods, and cover with water. Bring mixture to a boil, reduce heat, and simmer for 20 minutes. Remove from heat, cool slightly, then strain out the spices. Return the flavored water to the pot.

Over low heat, add the sugar and citric acid to the pot, stirring until the sugar is dissolved. Still over low heat, whisk in the arabic powder until it is dissolved. Remove from heat, place in a nonreactive container, and refrigerate until mixture is chilled.

Combine the syrups in a 1:1 ratio. (Any leftover syrup can be reserved for another use.) To make each soda, measure ¼ cup (60 mL) of syrup into each glass, top with ice and seltzer, and stir to incorporate.

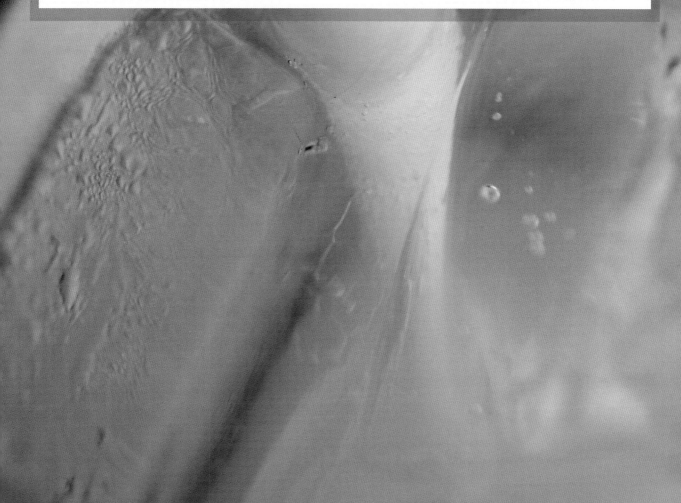

## MAINE SODAS, OLD AND NEW

In the tradition of Maine's iconic Moxie soda, a bittersweet brew created by Union's Dr. Augustin Thompson in 1884, a new wave of nonalcoholic beverages has swept the state. Many restaurants are making small batches of soda in-house, available by the glass, but there are also a wide variety of bottled refreshments.

Begun with Maine Root, an organic, fair-trade certified soda that is now available worldwide, there are several companies crafting artisan sodas around the state. Maine Root bottles its original root beer, as well as ginger beer, sarsaparilla, and blueberry and orange sodas. Green Bee makes its Lemon Sting with honey, lemon, and rosemary, and has recently launched Blueberry Dream, made from wild blueberries and honey. Capt'n Eli's, brewed by beer makers Shipyard Brewing Company, includes Strawberry Pop and Parrot Punch among its classic offerings. And of course Moxie can still be found bottled or in the bright-orange can. Try them all on tap at restaurants around Portland, or pick up a four-pack at groceries around the state.

# BLYTH AND BURROWS

26 Exchange Street
Portland, Maine
(207) 613-9070
*blythandburrows.com*
Owner: Joshua Miranda
Chef: Darci Pacewicz
Sous Chef: Nicholas Pacewicz

"In life honorable, in death glorious" is the tribute offered to captains Samuel Blyth and William Burrows at their namesake bar in the Old Port. The story of these rivals, both mortally wounded in a battle between their ships in Casco Bay during the War of 1812, and buried side by side in Portland's Eastern Cemetery, permeates this classic cocktail bar, whose decor is accented with weathered figureheads and other maritime treasures. Under the watchful eyes of Blyth and Burrows, whose portraits hang above the bar, carefully crafted cocktails are poured by some of the city's best veteran bartenders and topped with playful garnishes such as cutouts of ships, printed in edible ink on rice paper. From the kitchen, Executive Chef Darci Pacewicz and her husband, Sous Chef Nicholas Pacewicz, create beautiful, inventive dishes that emphasize sustainable local ingredients and complement the offerings from the space's raw bar.

Named 2018's Best New Cocktail Bar by both *Down East* magazine and *The Portland Phoenix*, Blyth and Burrows includes two bars that are accessible from Exchange Street and a third speakeasy, The Broken Dram, that can be reached either from an entrance in the alleyway off of Fore Street or through a false bookcase in the upper level of the bar. The menu here is highballs and drams, paired together and named after a different type of tragic duo: celebrity couples.

The cocktails below are assembled from several components, some of which must steep for several days before they are ready for use. They are worth the effort—make sure to plan ahead! Cream chargers, which use nitrous oxide to instantly whip cream and egg whites, are a common tool in commercial kitchens and can be ordered online. If you do not have one, you can whip the absinthe foam with a hand mixer, but it will break down and dissolve much more quickly.

At the restaurant, Chef Pacewicz serves her Poke Bao on black squid ink buns for a subtly briny taste and a vivid contrast of colors. Here, the recipe omits the squid ink, making the buns versatile for any filling. *Furikake* is a dry Japanese seasoning blend made of seaweed, sesame seeds, and flakes of dried fish. It can be found at Asian markets and in some grocery stores. Chef Pacewicz recommends Maine-made Ocean's Balance Spicy Seaweed Sprinkle, available in specialty markets and online.

It may take a few tries to become comfortable shaping your dumplings, but once they're cooked, even the practice ones will be delicious! Used in the Bourbon Mushroom Chicken Dumplings, black garlic is an Asian ingredient, made by aging garlic bulbs under carefully controlled temperature and humidity, until it becomes dark and sweetly tangy. Some chefs make their own black garlic, but it can be found online and in specialty markets. Mushroom powder, made from pulverized dried mushrooms, has been called "umami in a jar" and gives dishes body and depth. It is widely available in grocery stores and online. Ponzu sauce can be bought in the Asian section of most markets, or you can make your own (see Mr. Tuna's Garlic Ponzu, page 114). Note: When working with raw chicken, make sure to clean all surfaces and utensils thoroughly, and never taste the mixture before it has been cooked to 165°F.

# CALL ME ISHMAEL

(MAKES 1 GENEROUS COCKTAIL)

Absinthe Foam (see recipe below)

1½ ounces Persimmon-Infused Bourbon
    (see recipe below)

½ ounce Rittenhouse Rye

¼ ounce Dram Digestif Blend #2 (see recipe
    below)

¼ ounce persimmon syrup

3 dashes Owl & Whale Persimmon Bitters

## Absinthe Foam

2 ounces St. George Absinthe Verte

4 ounces simple syrup

4 ounces water

2 ounces lemon juice

5 dashes pimento or tiki bitters

3 egg whites

To make Absinthe Foam: In a ½ liter cream charger, with a single nitrous charge, combine all ingredients, adding the egg whites last. Shake hard for 30 seconds to fully blend ingredients, then chill in refrigerator for 30 minutes before use.

## Persimmon-Infused Bourbon

750 milliliters Buffalo Trace Bourbon

4 ounces dried persimmon

To make Persimmon-Infused Bourbon: In a large glass bottle, combine bourbon and dried persimmons. Allow to steep for at least 3 days before use.

## Dram Digestif Blend #2

375 milliliters Green Chartreuse

375 milliliters Yellow Chartreuse

375 milliliters Suze

To make the digestif blend: In a large glass bottle, combine all ingredients and gently stir. This blend can be used in cocktails or sipped on its own after a meal.

To assemble the drink: In a cocktail shaker over crushed ice, combine bourbon, rye, Dram Digestif Blend #2, persimmon syrup, and persimmon bitters. Shake until well blended, and strain into a cocktail glass. Top with Absinthe Foam and serve immediately.

# SHIP, CAPTAIN, CREW

(MAKES 1 GENEROUS COCKTAIL)

1½ ounces Dandelion-Infused Bourbon (see recipe below)

¼ ounce Smith and Cross Jamaica Rum

¼ ounce Clement Agricole

¼ ounce Montenegro Amaro

¼ ounce Dios Baco Amontillado Sherry

¼ ounce Lemongrass Syrup (see recipe below)

¼ ounce water

1 barspoon Spruce Tip Tincture (see recipe below)

## Dandelion-Infused Bourbon

750 milliliters Wild Turkey Bourbon

4 bags dandelion tea

**To make Dandelion-Infused Bourbon:** In a large glass bottle, combine bourbon and dandelion tea. Allow to steep for 3 days before use.

## Lemongrass Syrup

3 stalks lemongrass

1¼ cups water

2½ cups cane sugar

**To make Lemongrass Syrup:** In a small, nonreactive saucepan, combine lemongrass stalks and water and bring to a simmer for 10 to 15 minutes. Slowly add the sugar, stirring to combine. When sugar is dissolved, remove from heat and let cool before use.

## Spruce Tip Tincture

Wild foraged Maine spruce tips (available at farmers' markets and online)

Overproof neutral grain spirit, such as Everclear

**To make Spruce Tip Tincture:** In a large glass jar, soak foraged spruce tips in neutral grain spirit for one week before use.

**To assemble the drink:** In a cocktail shaker over crushed ice, combine all ingredients. Shake until well blended; strain into a cocktail glass.

# POKE BAO BUN

## (MAKES 8 SERVINGS)

Steamed Bao Buns (see recipe below)

1 pound sushi-grade tuna, cut into small cubes

Poke Sauce (see recipe below)

Napa Cabbage Slaw (see recipe below)

*Furikake* seasoning, to taste

### Steamed Bao Buns

1 tablespoon active yeast

1½ cups wrist-temperature water (80–90°F)

6 tablespoons sugar

4¼ cups bread flour

½ teaspoon baking soda

¼ teaspoon baking powder

3 tablespoons nonfat milk powder

2½ teaspoons kosher salt

2 tablespoons rendered duck fat

**To make Bao Buns:** In the bowl of a stand mixer, combine yeast, water, and sugar. Sift the bread flour over the yeast mixture, making sure to completely cover the top of the liquid. Sift the baking soda, baking powder, and nonfat milk powder over the top of the flour. Sprinkle salt over the top. With the hook attachment on low speed, mix for 1 minute. Add the duck fat, increase speed to medium-low, and mix for 8 minutes. Remove dough to a greased bowl and let rise in a warm, draft-free place for 90 minutes, or until doubled in size.

Divide dough into walnut-size pieces (25 grams) and shape into balls. Let rest, covered, for 30 minutes.

With a greased rolling pin, roll each lump of dough into a 4-inch oval. Place a chopstick in the middle of the oval and fold the bao bun in half so that the ends touch. Gently remove the chopstick and place the finished bao bun on a small piece of parchment paper. Cover and let rise for 35 to 40 minutes, until doubled in size.

Place bao buns in the basket of a bamboo steamer (or in the steamer insert over a saucepan of water) and cook over boiling water for 10 minutes, without removing the lid. When the bao buns are cooked, take the steamer from the pot and remove the lid. Fill and serve bao buns immediately, or allow to cool to room temperature before storing in a container in the refrigerator or freezer.

### Poke Sauce

¼ cup sriracha

Juice of one lemon

2 tablespoons sesame oil

½ cup mayonnaise

**To make Poke Sauce:** Place all ingredients in a bowl and whisk until well incorporated.

## Napa Cabbage Slaw

½ cup Napa cabbage, cut in a chiffonade

¼ cup seeded and julienned jalapeño

¼ cup green onion, cut on a dramatic bias

**To make Napa Cabbage Slaw:** In a medium-size bowl, toss all ingredients together.

**To assemble Poke Bao Buns:** Toss tuna cubes in Poke Sauce. On a steamed Bao Bun, place Napa Cabbage Slaw, a spoonful of dressed tuna, and a dash of *furikake* seasoning. Serve immediately.

---

# BOURBON MUSHROOM CHICKEN DUMPLING

(MAKES 8 SERVINGS)

1½ cups coarsely chopped Napa cabbage

1 stalk lemongrass, peeled and chopped

4 cloves garlic, peeled and trimmed

2 cloves black garlic, peeled

1 heaping teaspoon lemon zest

2-inch knob of fresh ginger, peeled and chopped

3 tablespoons soy sauce, divided

Small jalapeño, seeded and coarsely chopped

½ bunch scallions, trimmed and chopped

1¾ teaspoons sesame oil

1 pound ground chicken

1½ tablespoons mushroom powder

1 heaping teaspoon cornstarch, plus extra for dusting

1 teaspoon kosher salt

1 package wonton wrappers

Canola oil, for cooking the dumplings

Ponzu sauce, for serving

In the bowl of a food processor, pulse coarsely chopped Napa cabbage four times, making sure to leave some chunks in the mix. Line a colander or large bowl with cheesecloth and place chopped cabbage onto the cloth. Twist the cheesecloth around the cabbage and squeeze to expel extra moisture. Place cabbage in a clean, large bowl.

Place lemongrass, garlic, black garlic, lemon zest, and ginger into the bowl of the food processor with 1 tablespoon soy sauce; grind until the mixture becomes a fine paste. Empty the paste into the bowl with the cabbage, using a rubber scraper to clean the sides.

Place the jalapeño, scallions, remaining 2 tablespoons of soy sauce, and the sesame oil in the bowl of the food processor and pulse until chunky. Add mixture to the large bowl.

Using a rubber scraper or gloved hands (the ginger and jalapeño will irritate bare skin), mix all ingredients, adding ground chicken, cornstarch, mushroom powder, and kosher salt.

**To make the dumplings:** On a clean counter, arrange the packaged wonton wrappers, a small bowl of water, and a small bowl of cornstarch. Once you have opened the wonton wrappers, cover them with a cloth to ensure they don't dry out.

For each dumpling, place 1½ tablespoons of filling in the center of a wonton wrapper. Dip your finger into the water and run it along the edge of the wrapper, moistening the perimeter. Dry your fingers before continuing so that the wonton doesn't stick to them. Fold the wrapper in half, forming an even rectangle, and gently seal the dumpling. If any filling has moved to the edges, push it delicately back to the center.

Once the rectangle is sealed, arrange it so that the folded side (or spine) is facing away from you. Place a drop of water on the far left corner of the dumpling, then make a slight dent in the spine. Bring the corner to the middle of the spine, folding it at the dent to create a small crease. Place a drop of water on the far right corner of the dumpling and bring it to the middle, sealing the dough together and creating a dumpling that looks like it's hugging itself. Gently dust the bottom of the dumpling with cornstarch and place on a plate until ready to cook.

**To cook the dumplings:** In a nonstick pan over medium-high heat, place a small amount of canola oil. When the oil begins to shimmer, add the dumplings to the pan one at a time, making sure not to crowd the pan. Cook, uncovered, until the bottoms of the dumplings are a deep golden brown. With the lid at the ready, add 3 tablespoons of water to the pan and cover immediately, cooking for 1 minute. Remove pan from heat and let sit, covered, for another minute. Remove lid. All water should be evaporated, and the dumplings should be cooked through. Serve immediately with ponzu sauce for dipping.

# BOLSTER, SNOW & CO.

**The Francis Hotel**
**747 Congress Street**
**(207) 772-7496**
*Restaurant closed 2019.*
Owner: Anthony DeLois/Uncommon Hospitality
Chef: Nicholas Verdisco

Intimately set in the lower level of the boutique Francis Hotel, Bolster, Snow & Co. serves a gracious, seasonal menu of modern American cuisine in a charming setting. The fifteen-room hotel, in a landmark Victorian building in the Bramhall neighborhood of the West End, has been meticulously restored and renovated, and its parlor and front rooms, accented by contemporary furniture and local art, offer a cozy spot to perch with a cocktail. The main dining room, with tables and a few lucky seats at the bar of the open kitchen, allows for a view of Chef Nicholas Verdisco at work. A changing menu of locally sourced produce, meats, and seafood is steeped in the seasons, with a few unexpected twists. Duck is paired with summer peaches, broccoli rabe, and olives, while in spring, strawberries are matched with ricotta, radishes, and mint.

For this Asian-inspired broccoli salad, slice the crowns of broccoli as thinly as possible on a mandoline, working lengthwise on the stems to achieve a long, tender strip. Assemble the salad just before serving to ensure a perfect, slightly crisp texture. To toast sliced nuts and seeds, place in a dry skillet over medium heat, shaking gently for 3 to 5 minutes, or until lightly browned.

## BROCCOLI SALAD
(MAKES 8 SERVINGS)

8–10 medium-size broccoli crowns

⅔ cup almonds, lightly toasted and sliced

1 cup loosely packed fresh mint leaves

1 cup loosely packed fresh cilantro leaves (no stems)

3 tablespoons white sesame seeds, lightly toasted (optional)

**Dressing**

1 pinch chile flakes

2 cloves garlic, minced or pressed

1 scant cup freshly squeezed lime juice

⅔ cup fish sauce

1¼ teaspoons light brown sugar

Using a mandoline, slice the broccoli crowns lengthwise into thin strips (you should have roughly 6 cups). Place in a large bowl.

Combine dressing ingredients into a blender and pulse for 30 seconds, until thoroughly incorporated. Pour dressing over sliced broccoli and toss to coat. Let sit at room temperature for 10 to 15 minutes. Add sliced almonds and herbs and toss to combine. Divide among serving bowls, if desired, and garnish with toasted white sesame seeds.

# Central Provisions

**414 Fore Street**
**(207) 805-1085**
*central-provisions.com*
Chef/Owner: Chris Gould
Co-Owner: Paige Gould

Occupying the lower two levels of a Federal-style brick building at the corner of Fore and Dana Streets in the Old Port, Central Provisions celebrates the flavors and history of Maine, promising simply, in a sign that swings above the front door: "Good Food and Strong Drink." Steeped in the history of the city, the restaurant's name is taken from the origins of its building, constructed in 1828 as a storehouse for provisions for the fleet of ships serving the East India Trading Company. (At that time, Dana Street was called Central.) By the time chef/owner Chris Gould and his wife and business partner, Paige, bought the building, it had been through many incarnations, but the Goulds stripped the space back to its foundations, leaving intact the pulleys, trap doors, and other curiosities they found during renovations. The decor they've chosen for the restaurant complements the space and features the work of Maine artisans: tables made of reclaimed heartwood barn boards, and barstools forged by a local blacksmith.

The menu offerings of small plates are labeled Raw, Cold, Hot, and Sweet, and ingredients are identified by their provenance. At the long wooden bar, drinks range from craft cocktails with house-made bitters, punches for two, and nonalcoholic "Temperance Drinks" like shrubs and sodas.

Soon after it opened in 2014, Central Provisions was named one of the top ten new restaurants in the country by *Bon Appetit* magazine, and the following year, it was a finalist for the James Beard award for the Best New Restaurant of 2015. Since then, the pace has stayed bustling, and the Goulds have opened a second restaurant, Tipo (page 203).

Earthy and sweet, Hay Smoked Carrots with Honey Vinaigrette and Goat Cheese has been on the menu since Central Provisions opened. Chef Gould makes his own goat cheese, but you can substitute your favorite fresh chèvre. Sweet, spicy, and tart, the honey vinaigrette includes *verjus*, an acidic, vinegar-like condiment made from pressed green grapes, which is available at specialty markets and online. Beloved by chefs, Forum Chardonnay vinegar is a traditionally made Spanish vinegar, aged in oak and chestnut casks, which is also available at specialty markets and online.

To achieve the carrots' perfectly smoky flavor, a smoke box of smoldering hay is nestled among the carrots in a deep hotel pan. Make sure to buy hay that is clean and fresh and hasn't been treated with chemicals. Cast-iron home-size smoke boxes can be purchased online, as can deep (6-inch) hotel pans. When making this recipe, make sure to have plenty of ventilation in your kitchen!

# HAY-SMOKED CARROTS WITH HONEY VINAIGRETTE AND GOAT CHEESE
### (MAKES 8 SERVINGS)

## Honey Vinaigrette

Small piece star anise

3 black peppercorns

½ crumbled pod black cardamom

1 (2-inch) cinnamon stick

⅔ cup honey

5 sprigs fresh thyme

1 cup white *verjus*

1½ tablespoons chardonnay vinegar

⅓ cup grapeseed oil

Salt, to taste

**To make Honey Vinaigrette:** In a small pot over medium-high heat, toast the star anise, peppercorns, and cardamom until fragrant. Add cinnamon stick, honey, and thyme and bring to a boil until foamy. Remove from heat. Pour *verjus* into the hot honey mixture, cover, and steep until cinnamon stick is soft, at least 1 hour. Strain liquid, and blend with chardonnay vinegar and grapeseed oil. Season with salt to taste.

## Hay-Smoked Carrots

2½ pounds rainbow carrots, preferably organic

4 tablespoons unsalted butter

1 cup fresh hay, preferably organic

½ cinnamon sticks

½ piece star anise

Freshly ground black pepper, to taste

Salt, to taste

**To make Hay-Smoked Carrots:** Preheat oven to 350°F. Thoroughly wash and trim carrots, cutting them into roughly uniform lengths if they are of varying sizes. In a rondeau pan or deep skillet over medium-high heat, melt the butter. Add carrots and cook, stirring occasionally, until they begin to caramelize, about 15 minutes. Transfer carrots to a deep hotel pan.

Place hay, cinnamon sticks, star anise, and pepper into a small (8 x 5 inch) smoke box, and nestle it among the carrots in the hotel pan. Making sure that your kitchen is well ventilated, ignite the hay, and blow until it smolders and smokes. Cover the smoke box and pan with foil, and then place in the preheated oven. Smoke until all carrots are tender. Note: Each carrot may have a different cook time, depending on variations in size, so check frequently and remove carrots as they are fully cooked. Make sure to reignite the smoking mixture every time you check the carrots.

When all carrots are fully cooked, place them on a tray or sheet pan to cool.

### The Dish

8 ounces fresh chèvre goat cheese

Zest of ½ lemon

½ c. unsalted butter, for sautéing carrots

Smoked sea salt, to taste

6 sprigs fresh thyme

¼ cup toasted pistachios, crushed, for garnish

Sliced chives, for garnish

**To assemble the dish:** In a small bowl, mix together fresh chèvre, lemon zest, and smoked sea salt. Place the cheese on a serving platter, spreading to make a bed for the carrots. Just before serving, sauté the Hay-Smoked Carrots in butter, cooking until they are golden brown and thoroughly warmed. Add fresh thyme leaves to the hot pan at the end of cooking to impart a fresh, herby flavor. Strain off excess butter and place carrots in a large bowl with the Honey Vinaigrette. Toss to coat. Place carrots on top of the chèvre mixture, and garnish with crushed pistachios, sliced chives, and a sprinkling of smoked salt.

# CORN AND LOBSTER FRITTERS WITH SAFFRON AIOLI

(MAKES 8 SERVINGS)

## Saffron Aioli

1 tablespoon canola oil

⅓ cup brunoise (⅛-inch dice) shallots

1 clove garlic, minced

1 tablespoon saffron

Pinch of salt

1⅓ cup mayonnaise

⅓ cup buttermilk

**To make the saffron aioli:** In a small skillet over low heat, heat the canola oil. Add the shallots, garlic, saffron, and salt. Sweat the mixture over low heat until shallots and garlic are fragrant and translucent, but not browning. Remove from the skillet and puree in a food processor or blender until smooth.

In a medium-size bowl, whisk together the mayonnaise and buttermilk. Add the shallot and garlic puree and mix until smooth. Refrigerate until ready to use.

## Corn and Lobster Fritters

2 cups flour

1 cup cornmeal

⅓ cup sugar

2 teaspoons baking powder

2 teaspoons salt

⅔ cup sliced scallions

⅓ cup chopped cooked bacon

4 large ears sweet corn, kernels cut from cob

⅓ cup brown butter

1⅓ cups diced cooked lobster meat

Canola oil, for frying

Sliced scallions, for garnish

**To make the fritters:** In a large bowl, combine the flour, cornmeal, sugar, baking powder, and salt, whisking to blend. In a separate large bowl, stir together the scallions, bacon, corn kernels, brown butter, and cooked lobster meat. Pour the wet ingredients into the dry, using a rubber scraper to clean the sides of the bowl. Mix until just incorporated—be careful not to overmix.

Heat canola oil in a deep fryer or a deep skillet over high heat, until oil registers 350°F. Using a ¾-ounce scoop, slip balls of the fritter mixture into the hot oil, frying until golden, about 3 minutes.

Serve corn and lobster fritters with saffron aioli, and garnish with sliced scallions.

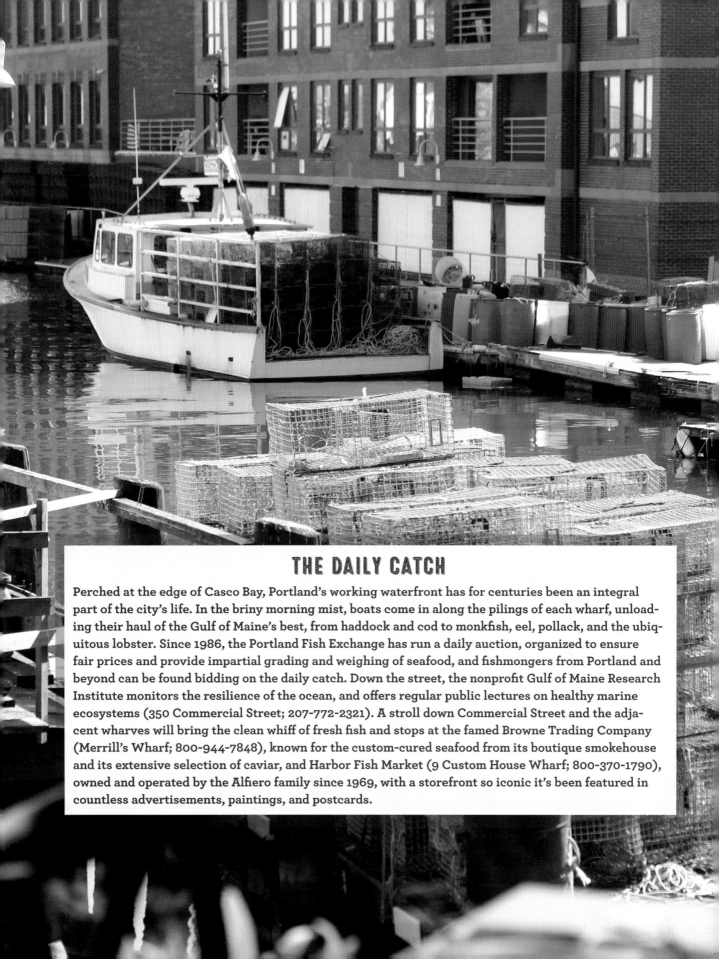

## THE DAILY CATCH

Perched at the edge of Casco Bay, Portland's working waterfront has for centuries been an integral part of the city's life. In the briny morning mist, boats come in along the pilings of each wharf, unloading their haul of the Gulf of Maine's best, from haddock and cod to monkfish, eel, pollack, and the ubiquitous lobster. Since 1986, the Portland Fish Exchange has run a daily auction, organized to ensure fair prices and provide impartial grading and weighing of seafood, and fishmongers from Portland and beyond can be found bidding on the daily catch. Down the street, the nonprofit Gulf of Maine Research Institute monitors the resilience of the ocean, and offers regular public lectures on healthy marine ecosystems (350 Commercial Street; 207-772-2321). A stroll down Commercial Street and the adjacent wharves will bring the clean whiff of fresh fish and stops at the famed Browne Trading Company (Merrill's Wharf; 800-944-7848), known for the custom-cured seafood from its boutique smokehouse and its extensive selection of caviar, and Harbor Fish Market (9 Custom House Wharf; 800-370-1790), owned and operated by the Alfiero family since 1969, with a storefront so iconic it's been featured in countless advertisements, paintings, and postcards.

# MAINE POTATOES

From All-Blue to Onaway, Katahdin to Kennebec, Adirondack Red to Swedish Peanut Fingerlings, Maine potatoes come in all colors, shapes, and sizes. For many years the leading potato producer in the country, Maine still takes pride in her spuds. Thriving in the cool climate and fertile soil of northern Aroostook County, potatoes have been one of Maine's staple foods for centuries and were a leading export since their introduction in the early 1800s. Between 1928 and 1958, Maine grew more potatoes than any other state in the nation, and though production has declined over the past fifty years, Maine potatoes are still beloved by chefs and renowned for their earthy flavor and diverse varieties. Look for them by name on menus and at markets around town.

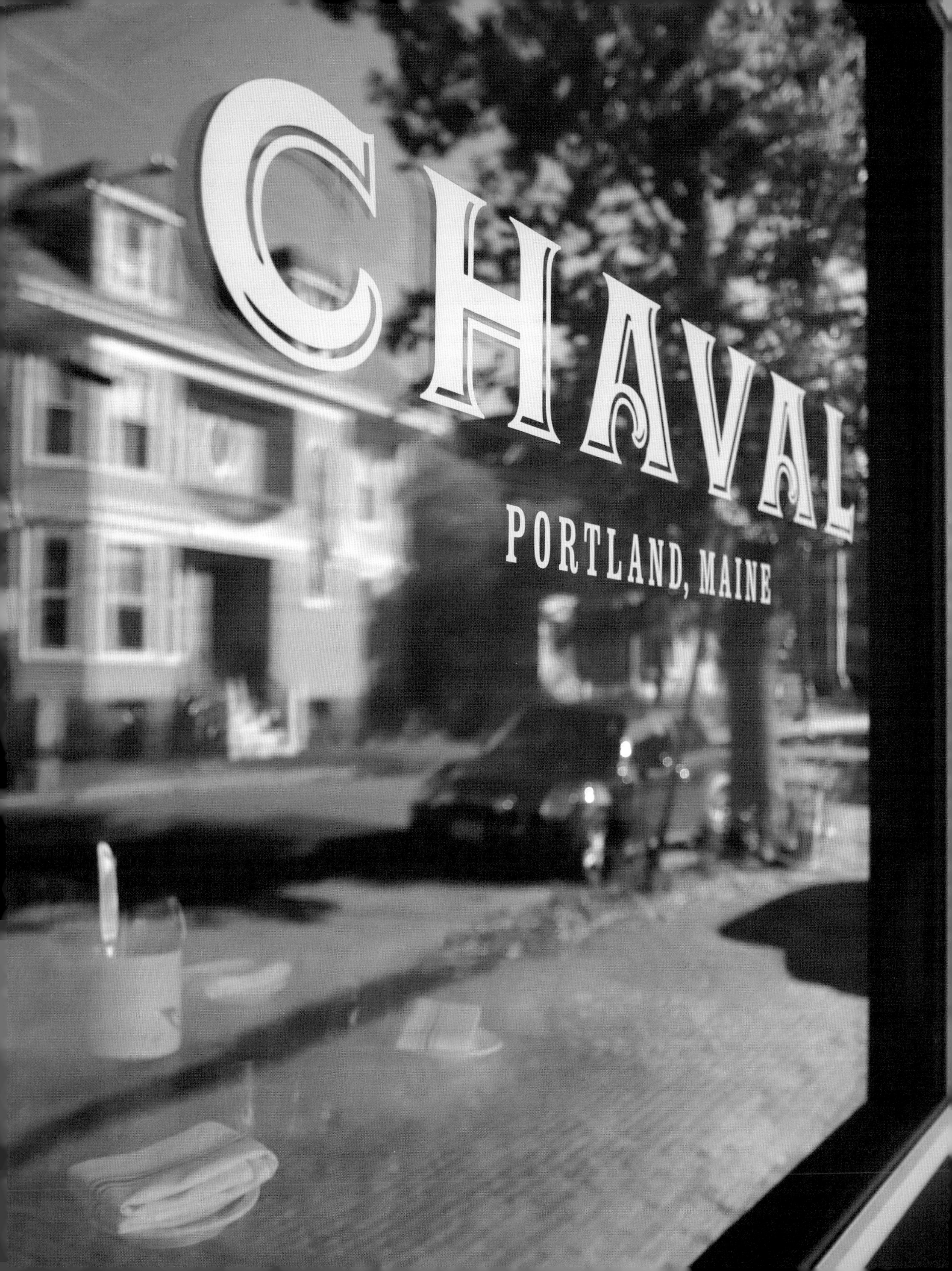
CHAVAL
PORTLAND, MAINE

# CHAVAL

**58 Pine Street**
**(207) 772-1110**
*chavalmaine.com*
Chef/Owners: Damian Sansonetti and Ilma Jeil Lopez

This cozy neighborhood brasserie in the West End is the second restaurant from Chefs Damian Sansonetti and Ilma Jeil Lopez. Here, the couple, who also own Piccolo (page 131), serve hearty Spanish and French food in a warm atmosphere: Neighborhood regulars take a seat at the long, poured concrete bar for *patatas bravas* and a glass of Tempranillo, while Sunday brunch packs the house with families and groups that spill onto the patio when weather allows. So beloved is Chaval that its mismatched china, a feature of each tabletop, is often donated by loyal patrons.

The menu features classic dishes that nod to Chef Sansonetti's time at New York's famed Bar Boulud, such as the rich, long-braised coq au vin, meaty beef tartare and bone marrow, duck rillettes, and octopus *a la plancha*, alongside more casual offerings like the house burger, made from local beef and served on a homemade black pepper brioche bun. Desserts from two-time James Beard semifinalist Chef Lopez range from crispy churros in hot chocolate sauce to the Spanish Sundae: smoky serrano ham ice cream served with chocolate cake and bacon caramel.

The recipe below is a hearty, subtly flavored take on a French classic. When preparing, make sure to allot yourself 24 hours to marinate the chicken in advance.

## COQ AU VIN
(MAKES 6 SERVINGS)

9 chicken legs

9 chicken thighs

2 stalks celery, sliced

1 bulb garlic, sliced in half horizontally

1 medium Spanish onion, sliced

1 medium carrot, peeled and sliced

1 sachet (see recipe below)

1 pound smoked North Country slab bacon, cut into ¼-inch pieces

1 cup pearl onions, peeled

4 cups small button or crimini mushrooms, cleaned and trimmed

2–3 organic heirloom carrots, cut into thick rounds

3 cups dry red wine

¼ cup all-purpose flour

Salt

Freshly ground black pepper

¼ cup olive oil

4–6 cups unsalted chicken/veal/beef stock (warmed and reserved)

### Sachet

4 sprigs thyme

2 bay leaves

1 teaspoon cracked black pepper

**To make the sachet:** Place all the ingredients in the center of a square of cheesecloth. Gather the corners and tie the bundle together with kitchen twine, forming a little purse of herbs.

**For the Coq Au Vin:** Place chicken, celery, garlic, Spanish onions, carrots, and sachet in a large, nonreactive container. Cover and reserve in refrigerator until needed.

In a large skillet over medium-high heat, cook the bacon until crisp. Remove from pan and place on paper towels to drain. In the same skillet, add pearl onions and cook, stirring occasionally, for 6 minutes. Remove with a slotted spoon.

Using separate large squares of cheesecloth, make individual bundles of the cooked bacon, sautéed pearl onions, trimmed mushrooms, and sliced carrots. Tie each bundle with kitchen twine. Place the bundles in the container with the chicken and cover with wine. Marinate in the refrigerator for 24 hours.

Heat oven to 325°F.

Drain marinade from chicken into a nonreactive saucepan set over medium heat. Cook until liquid is reduced by half. Set aside and reserve.

Using paper towels, pat dry the chicken pieces. Place flour in a shallow bowl and dredge the chicken until each piece is lightly coated. Season the chicken with salt and pepper. Set aside and reserve.

Place olive oil in a large Dutch oven, and heat over medium-high. Add the chicken in a single layer, cooking in batches, if necessary. Turn chicken pieces while cooking to ensure browning on all sides. Remove from oil and set aside.

Place the marinated celery, garlic, onion, and carrot into the Dutch oven. Reduce heat to medium and cook until vegetables are softened, about 6 minutes. Add the reduced wine, chicken, sachet, and bundles of bacon, pearl onions, mushrooms, and carrots. Add stock to the pot and bring to a boil. Cover with a round of parchment paper and place in the oven; braise until tender, about an hour. Remove from the oven and let stand for 20 minutes.

Remove the chicken and bundles from the Dutch oven and strain the remaining liquid into a large, clean saucepan. Discard solids that have been strained from the sauce. Over medium-high heat, reduce the sauce until it coats the back of a spoon. When ready to serve, add chicken to the sauce. Untie the bundles of bacon, onions, mushrooms, and carrots and add to the pot. Adjust seasonings to taste, then cook over medium heat until warmed through.

To serve, place three pieces of chicken in each serving bowl. Cover with sauce, bacon, onions, mushrooms, and carrots. It is traditional to serve coq au vin with baked fingerling potatoes cut into pieces and tossed with butter and parsley. Note: Coq au vin can be made a full day or two ahead of time and reserved. In fact, it's better to let the flavors come together and marry well.

# Drifters Wife

59 Washington Avenue
(207) 805-1336
*drifterswife.com*
Co-Owners: Orenda and Peter Hale
Chef: Ben Jackson

When Orenda and Peter Hale opened a wine bar at the front of their natural wine store, Maine and Loire, they chose Chef Ben Jackson, a colleague from their days in restaurants in New York City, to helm the kitchen. Their collaboration, Drifters Wife, soon became a beloved part of Portland's food scene. Since opening in 2016, the restaurant, which has expanded to a larger space next door, has served a small, hyper-local menu, emphasizing the elements that drew them all to Maine: its rugged coastline, fertile woods, and deep agricultural roots. The offerings change nightly and showcase foraged foods, as well as farmed. Sweetly earthy dulse butter, made with seaweed gathered off Maine's coast, complements tangy sourdough, and foraged mushrooms, nuts, and spring ramps and fiddleheads appear regularly on the menu. Malabi, a Middle Eastern milk pudding that is one of the restaurant's signature desserts, is served with a changing topping of crushed nuts and seasonal stewed fruits. Natural wines are served by both the glass and the bottle.

Chef Jackson's simple approach has earned high praise: In 2017, Drifters Wife was a semifinalist for the James Beard award for Best New Restaurant, and in 2018 it was named one of the top ten restaurants in America by *Bon Appetit*.

# PORK COPPA WITH ENGLISH PEAS, DILL MAYO, AND ICEBERG LETTUCE

At Drifters Wife, slow-cooked coppa is a beloved entree that appears regularly on the menu. When there are leftovers, they make their way into this fresh summer salad, made with local iceberg lettuce and English peas from Steelbow Farms. If coppa isn't available, Chef Ben Jackson suggests substituting "anything hammy from your local butcher."

(MAKES 4 SERVINGS)

½ cup shelled English peas, shells reserved

2 heads iceberg lettuce, torn

4 teaspoons freshly squeezed lemon juice

8 teaspoons extra virgin olive oil

8 ounces sliced smoked ham

½ cup Creamy Dill Dressing (see recipe below)

Salt and freshly ground black pepper, to taste

In a medium-size saucepan, combine reserved pea shells with enough water to cover by 3 inches. Bring to a boil, then reduce to a simmer and cook for 30 minutes. Let cool slightly, then strain into a clean saucepan. Discard the shells and salt the broth generously (Chef Jackson notes that it should taste "like Maine seawater"). Return the broth to the stove, add the shelled peas, and cook them until they are bright green and just tender. When they are at the desired consistency, plunge the peas immediately into an ice bath to stop them from cooking.

In a large bowl, toss the torn iceberg lettuce with the lemon juice, olive oil, and a sprinkle of salt. To assemble the salad, place a bed of lettuce on each plate, then divide the blanched peas and smoked ham evenly among the plates. Dress with the Creamy Dill Dressing and top with salt and freshly ground pepper, to taste.

## Creamy Dill Dressing

(MAKES 1 QUART)

½ cup salted capers

5 egg yolks

6 tablespoons Dijon mustard

6 tablespoons cider vinegar

Juice of 2 lemons

½ cup finely chopped chives

⅓ cup brunoise (⅛-inch dice) shallots

¼ cup finely chopped dill

Pinch of chile de árbol

To make Creamy Dill Dressing: Prepare the salted capers by soaking them in fresh water, draining, then rinsing three times to remove excess salt. Pat drained capers dry, and roughly chop them.

In a large bowl, whisk together all ingredients until they form a thick, rich dressing. Use immediately, or refrigerate for up to 3 days.

# BANGS ISLAND MUSSEL TOAST WITH AIOLI, GREEN GARLIC, SUNGOLD TOMATOES, AND BASIL

(MAKES 4 SERVINGS)

2 dozen Bangs Island mussels, cleaned

2–3 cups dry white wine

2 cloves garlic, smashed

4 sprigs thyme

2 sprigs rosemary

4 leeks, trimmed and grilled (green garlic can be substituted)

1 cup sungold tomatoes, halved

2 cups chopped fresh mixed herbs: parsley, chives, scallions, basil, cilantro

Sea salt and freshly ground black pepper, to taste

4 slices sourdough (or other naturally leavened) bread

Extra virgin olive oil, for brushing

Aioli (see recipe below)

Check the mussels to make sure that they are clean and tightly closed. In a large pot over medium-high heat, combine white wine with garlic cloves, thyme, and rosemary. Bring the mixture to a boil and add mussels, steaming until they just pop. Remove the mussels from their shells and toss them with the leeks, tomatoes, mixed herbs, and steaming juices. Adjust seasoning to taste.

Brush the bread with olive oil and fry quickly in a skillet set over medium-high heat. To serve, place each slice of bread on a plate. Spread a generous amount of aioli onto each slice of bread, then spoon the mussel mixture over each piece, dividing evenly among the plates.

## Aioli

(MAKES 3 CUPS)

2 large garlic cloves

1 teaspoon sea salt

2 egg yolks

Juice of ½ lemon

¼ teaspoon Dijon mustard (optional)

2 cups canola oil

To make Aioli: Peel and finely chop the garlic. Add sea salt and, using a mortar and pestle, grind the mixture into a smooth-textured paste.

In the bowl of a food processor, combine garlic paste with egg yolks, lemon juice, and optional Dijon mustard. Blend until mixture is thoroughly combined. With the food processor on, slowly drizzle in the oil until the mixture becomes thick and creamy. If it's too thick, thin the sauce with a few drops of water. Leftover aioli can be stored in the refrigerator for up to a week.

# DUTCH'S

**28 Prebble Street**
**207-761-2900**
*dutchsportland.com*
Chef/Owners: Ian and Lucy Dutch

On a stretch of Prebble Street dotted with thrift stores and an arcade, in an open, cheery space with a vintage vacationland vibe, Dutch's serves made-from-scratch breakfast and lunch six days a week. Married chef/owners Ian and Lucy Dutch share the kitchen—she trained as a baker, he's a graduate of the Culinary Institute of America. The two put their own stamp on classics, serving up breakfast hashes, benedicts, muffins, and grits alongside avocado toasts and brioche cinnamon buns. Lunch is nostalgia brought to life: A sandwich of peanut butter and strawberry jam on homemade country white bread is served warm, and grilled cheese and tuna melts are slathered in mayonnaise and cheese and griddled to perfection. A case full of gooey bars, frosted cake squares, and other indulgent pastries round out the meal. If you're feeling bold, get a "mystery box" to go.

# WILD MAINE BLUEBERRY MUFFINS

### (MAKES 30 MUFFINS)

**Muffins**

2 cups vegetable or canola oil

3¼ cups milk

6 eggs

3 tablespoons vanilla

8 cups all purpose flour

3 cups light brown sugar

3 tablespoons baking powder

2 teaspoons salt

Scant 8 cups wild Maine blueberries, fresh or frozen

Crumble topping (see recipe below)

Blueberry Jam (see recipe below)

Preheat oven to 325 degrees. Lightly grease 30 muffin cups.

In a large bowl or oversized glass measuring cup, whisk together the oil, milk, eggs, and vanilla until fully incorporated. In a separate large bowl, whisk together the flour, brown sugar, baking powder, and salt. Pour the liquid mixture into the dry, and stir briefly to combine. *Be careful not to overmix.* Stir in the blueberries.

Using an ice cream scoop or large spoon, scoop batter into prepared muffin cups. Top each muffin with a generous amount of Crumble Topping and bake for 12 minutes. Rotate the pans and return them to the oven to bake for 12 minutes more, until the topping is a toasty light golden brown. Serve with a generous dollop of Blueberry Jam.

## Crumble Topping

4 cups all purpose flour

½ cup plus 2 tablespoons sugar

½ cup plus 2 tablespoons light brown sugar

1¼ teaspoons cinnamon

¾ cup milk powder

1½ cups almond meal

1 tablespoon salt

2⅓ cups unsalted butter

In a large bowl, combine all ingredients and mix well with your hands until all of the butter has been worked in and crumbs begin to form. Lay the crumbs out on a rimmed sheet tray and refrigerate for several hours to chill. Store any leftover crumble topping in an airtight container in the refrigerator.

## Blueberry Jam

(MAKES 2 QUARTS)

10 cups frozen blueberries

3 cups sugar

2½ teaspoons salt

Juice of 1 lemon

½ cup sugar

1 tablespoon pectin

In the top of a large double boiler set over simmering water, combine the blueberries, sugar, salt, and lemon juice, and cook slowly until the juices begin to release, 2 hours. Transfer the mixture to a large, heavy-bottomed pot. In a small bowl, mix the remaining sugar with the pectin and sprinkle over the jam. Stir well to incorporate, and simmer over low heat for 15–25 minutes, until the jam begins to thicken and coats the back of a spoon.

---

# POPOVERS BENEDICT

This twist on traditional eggs Benedict is served on a freshly made popover.

(MAKES 12 POPOVERS)

Popovers (see recipe below)

Hollandaise (see recipe below)

White Wine Reduction (see recipe below)

2 dozen eggs

Vinegar, for poaching eggs

2 large bunches kale

6 tomatoes, sliced

## Popovers

12 tablespoons canola oil, separated

Scant 4 cups whole milk

6 tablespoons plus 1 teaspoon unsalted butter

8 eggs

3 cups all-purpose flour

2 teaspoons salt

2 teaspoons freshly ground black pepper

**To make the popovers:** Preheat oven to 450°F. Prepare muffin tins by filling each cup with 1 tablespoon of canola oil. Place muffin tins in preheated oven for 10 minutes. Remove muffin tins from the oven, and reduce temperature to 400°F.

Place milk and butter in an oversized glass measuring cup or other microwave-safe bowl, and microwave on high for 4 minutes, until milk has scalded and butter has melted. Place remaining ingredients in a large bowl, and pour warmed milk mixture over them. Using a stick blender, blend mixture until it is completely smooth and the consistency of thick cream. Pour batter into hot muffin tins, filling each cup to the top. Bake for 40 minutes, until tops have popped.

## Hollandaise

(MAKES 1 QUART)

⅓ cup white wine reduction (see recipe below)

13 egg yolks

1½ teaspoons salt

2 cups unsalted butter, melted

1½ teaspoons hot sauce

1½ teaspoons Worcestershire sauce

¾ teaspoon lemon juice

**To make Hollandaise:** In the top of a double boiler set over simmering water, combine white wine reduction, egg yolks, and salt, and whisk until the yolks start to thicken and form ribbons.

Remove from heat, take the top off the double boiler pot below, and slowly stir in the melted butter. Stir in the hot sauce, Worcestershire sauce, and lemon juice, and adjust to taste before serving.

## White Wine Reduction

3⅓ cups white wine

¾ cup plus 1½ tablespoons white wine vinegar

1 teaspoon black peppercorns

1 teaspoon whole coriander

2 bay leaves

⅔ cup shallots, sliced

**To make White Wine Reduction:** In a medium-sized saucepan, combine all the ingredients, and set over high heat. Bring mixture to a boil, and cook, stirring occasionally, until it is reduced by half. Strain reduction through a seive, and discard peppercorns, coriander, bay leaves, and shallots before use.

## Poached Eggs and Assembly

Bring a saucepan of water to a simmer, and add 1 tablespoon of distilled vinegar for every quart of water. Crack each egg into a small bowl before gently slipping it into the simmering water. Poach eggs until the whites are set and the yolk is still runny.

**To prepare the kale and tomato:** Clean and trim the kale, discarding stems and tearing leaves into large pieces. Bring a large pot of salted water to the boil over high heat, and quickly blanch the kale, until it is bright green and slightly softened. Remove kale from water with a slotted spoon, and pat dry with a clean kitchen towel or paper towel.

Place a saute pan or griddle on high heat and lightly drizzle with extra virgin olive oil. Place the tomato slices in the oil to warm, flipping once.

**To assemble:** Cut open each popover and layer on about an ounce of kale and two slices of tomato on each side. Place one poached egg in each half, and top with a generous spoonful of hollandaise. Serve immediately.

# EAUX

90 Exchange Street
(207) 835-0283
*eauxportland.com*
Chef/Owner: Evan Richardson

After just one summer as a mobile food unit serving up authentic Louisiana cuisine, Chef Evan Richardson, a Cajun transplant, and his wife, Genevieve, knew that Portland hungered for the big, comforting flavors they had to offer. When a space became available in a busy stretch of Exchange Street, they jumped at the chance, and with the help of family and friends, the two were able to transform it in just a couple of months. The hand-built banquettes and bar are simple and rustic, with tables just wide enough to tuck in an extra plate to share. During the build-out, the couple realized there was no space for a walk-in refrigerator in the kitchen, so everything is made from scratch daily: fluffy biscuits, rich gravy, crispy fried chicken, shrimp and grits, and long-simmered gumbos and beans. Menu favorites are livened up with unexpected twists, seasonal Maine ingredients, and a dash or two from the bottles of Crystal Hot Sauce that adorn every table. At the bar, cocktails play with riffs on Louisiana culture—Sweet Tea Pain is a summer favorite, while the Chicorée and Cream pairs cream soda with bitter Blue Lion Chicorée liqueur. Come late at night and you'll find the place packed with staff from neighboring restaurants—the highest praise around!

A Louisiana pantry staple, blackening seasoning can be bought premixed, or it can be made from scratch by combining paprika, garlic powder, onion powder, thyme, ground black pepper, cayenne, basil, and oregano. The versatile spice blend can be used to give a Cajun kick to seafood, meat, poultry, and vegetables. Store at room temperature in an airtight container.

# RED BEANS AND RICE

(MAKES 8 SERVINGS)

2 tablespoons rendered pork fat or shortening

8 garlic cloves, minced

½ pound black cherry wood smoked bacon, cubed

3 stalks celery, diced

1 medium onion, diced

1½ bell peppers, diced

2 small bay leaves

8 stems fresh thyme

¼ cup blackening seasoning, premixed
   or homemade

⅓ cup dry vermouth

2 quarts kidney beans, soaked overnight

1 tablespoon Worcestershire sauce

2 quarts chicken stock

Crystal Hot Sauce, to taste

Salt and pepper, to taste

4 cups water

2 cups jasmine rice

Sliced scallions and hot peppers, for garnish
   (optional)

Note: Salt the dish lightly after each addition to season every component of the beans.

In a large pot over medium heat, melt pork fat or shortening. Add garlic and bacon and cook until fragrant. Increase heat to medium-high and add celery, onion, bell peppers, bay leaves, and fresh thyme. Salt to taste and cook until "fond"—the caramelization of the sugars in the mixture—begins to form on the bottom of the pan. Add blackening seasoning to the pan and toast the spices, stirring frequently, until fragrant. Deglaze the pan with dry vermouth and reduce the mixture in the pot. Add soaked kidney beans, Worcestershire sauce, 1 quart of the chicken stock, and hot sauce and pepper to taste. Taste the broth as it comes to a slow boil; adjust salt and pepper, noting that black pepper is a pivotal ingredient in Creole cooking, and its flavor should come through. Reduce heat to a simmer and stew down, adding chicken stock as necessary, until beans are fully tender. Continue cooking until liquid is the consistency of a medium roux or baked beans.

In a separate large pot, bring water to a boil. Stir in rice and bring back to a boil, lowering heat to a simmer and cooking, covered, over low heat for 15 minutes. Turn off the heat and leave rice covered for an additional 15 minutes.

Serve beans over rice, garnished with scallions and spicy peppers, if desired.

# DROP BISCUITS AND ANDOUILLE GRAVY

(MAKES 8 SERVINGS)

## Drop Biscuits

2 cups all-purpose flour

2 teaspoons baking powder

½ teaspoon baking soda

1 teaspoon granulated sugar

¾ teaspoon salt

½ cup (1 stick) unsalted butter

1 cup buttermilk, chilled

2 bunches chives, snipped into ½-inch lengths

**To make Drop Biscuits:** Preheat oven to 475°F. In a medium-size bowl, combine dry ingredients. In a small saucepan over low heat, melt the butter. Pour cold buttermilk into a large mixing bowl and add melted butter, mixing quickly to form small coagulations. Sift dry ingredients into the buttermilk mixture and fold in chives, being careful not to overmix. Divide dough into equal portions and scoop onto a greased cookie sheet, making sure not to crowd the sheet. Bake for 12 minutes, rotating pan midway through, until biscuits are lightly browned.

## Andouille Gravy

2 pounds andouille sausage, cut into 1-inch pieces

Approximately ½ cup rendered pork fat
   or shortening

½ cup all-purpose flour

1 quart beef stock

1 quart milk

Worcestershire sauce, to taste

Crystal hot sauce, to taste

Black pepper, to taste

Note: The amount of pork fat needed may vary based on the fat rendered from the andouille. Between the two ingredients, you will need ½ cup of fat.

**To make the Andouille Gravy:** In a large, heavy-bottomed pan over low heat, heat andouille, rendering as much fat as possible from the pieces. Remove sausage pieces and set aside. Add enough pork fat to make ½ cup, and whisk in flour. Cook thoroughly to a blonde roux, about 5 minutes. (The color of the roux may vary, depending on the andouille.)

   In a separate medium saucepan, combine beef stock and milk and warm over low heat. Slowly add mixture to the roux, whisking until it is fully incorporated; allow to simmer for 30 to 45 minutes. Return cooked sausage to the gravy, stirring to incorporate, and season heavily with Worcestershire sauce, hot sauce, and black pepper. Serve over Drop Biscuits. You can add poached or fried eggs, if desired.

# BANANAS FOSTER

(MAKES 4 SERVINGS)

2 ripe bananas

6 tablespoons dark rum

¼ cup freshly squeezed lemon juice

2–3 tablespoons brown sugar

Pinch of salt

4 tablespoons unsalted butter, separated

4 thick slices pound cake, lightly toasted, for serving

Pecans, for garnish

Note: This dish is very time-sensitive and should be made immediately before serving. The bananas will turn out differently if the instructions are not followed to the letter.

Slice bananas lengthwise and, in a skillet over medium-high heat, sear until cut side is lightly browned. Add rum and begin to reduce in the pan, then add lemon juice, and finally brown sugar (adding sugar too early risks crystalizing it). Fully reduce the mixture until large bubbles begin to form, then add a pinch of salt. Remove from heat and add butter, 1 tablespoon at a time, until the sauce is fully emulsified and is the rich color of caramel. Serve bananas and sauce over toasted slices of pound cake, and garnish with pecans.

- 7·GRAIN -
BREAD

# Forage

123 Washington Avenue
(207) 274-6800
and
180 Lisbon Street
Lewiston, Maine
(207) 333-6840
*foragemarket.com*
Baker/Owner: Allen Smith

The original Forage Market opened in 2012 in downtown Lewiston during a culinary renaissance that brought craft breweries and farm-to-table restaurants to Maine's second-largest city. The Lewiston space, warm with reclaimed woods, thrift-store china, and counter stools made from salvaged tractor seats, was dual purpose. In the front it held a grocery market selling locally sourced foods, and in back was a bakery featuring handcrafted bagels, made with a long-rising dough naturally leavened by a wild yeast starter, coated in a thick layer of seeds or crunchy salt, and baked in a wood-fired oven in the building's stone cellar. The bagels were an immediate hit, and soon the grocery shelves were replaced by more vintage Formica tables, as the bakery and cafe expanded. By 2016, an article in *Saveur* magazine had suggested that the best bagels in America were being crafted at Forage.

Six years after opening, Forage expanded its reach to Portland, opening a second location on a busy stretch of inner Washington Avenue. The commitment to local growers and producers continues, and in addition to the locally sourced ingredients on the cafe menu, the Portland space includes a flower market operated by Scarborough's Broadturn Farm. Owner and self-taught baker Allen Smith credits years spent in a lab studying plant evolution for his style of baking: meticulous; open to mistakes, which he calls "the source of the best discoveries"; and always in search of learning opportunities and process improvement. In his Portland location, this has meant the construction of a Spanish rotating-deck oven that has taken Forage's wood-fired bagels to a new level.

The Cranberry Bran Muffin is a menu favorite, made with organic local cranberries and a secret ingredient: banana puree, which keeps the muffin moist. Coarse wheat bran is available in the baking section of most grocers and at natural foods stores.

The 7-Grain Bread is used extensively in Forage's cafe service. A cooked porridge of Champlain Mills organic 7-grain cereal is mixed into the dough, and these cooked grains, with the enrichment of a little oil and honey, give the bread a tender and springy crumb that keeps well. A poolish, also called a sponge, is a prefermentation of flour, water, and yeast that brings a richer, more complex flavor to the dough. If you would like to make the bread in a single day, simply substitute the same amount of water and bread flour and omit the ⅛ teaspoon of yeast.

# CRANBERRY BRAN MUFFINS

(MAKES 2 DOZEN MUFFINS)

2 cups all-purpose flour

1½ teaspoons baking powder

1½ teaspoons cinnamon

½ teaspoon baking soda

2¼ cups coarse wheat bran (Bob's Red Mill)

1½ teaspoons kosher salt

½ cup very ripe banana

1 large egg

¾ cup, plus 3 tablespoons canola oil

½ cup, plus 3 tablespoons brown sugar

3 tablespoons molasses

1⅜ cups buttermilk

1¼ teaspoons pure vanilla extract

2 cups cranberries, frozen

Demerara or sanding sugar, for sprinkling

Preheat oven to 350°F. Line two muffin tins with cupcake liners.

In a large bowl, combine all dry ingredients, whisking to incorporate.

In a separate large bowl, mash banana with egg, oil, brown sugar, and molasses. Whisk mixture to emulsify. Stir in buttermilk and vanilla, mixing well.

Using a rubber spatula or wooden spoon, stir dry ingredients into banana mixture, mixing until all the dry ingredients are incorporated. Stir in frozen cranberries.

Spoon batter into prepared muffin tins, filling almost to the top (these muffins do not rise much). Top with a sprinkling of sugar. Bake for 50 to 60 minutes, until a cake tester inserted into the center comes out clean.

# 7-GRAIN BREAD

(MAKES 3 LOAVES)

½ cup water, at 88°F

1 cup bread flour

⅛ teaspoon dry yeast

1¼ cups prepared 7-grain hot cereal (see recipe below)

2½ cups boiling water

¾ cup, plus 2 tablespoons water

2 tablespoons, plus 2 teaspoons honey

⅓ cup canola oil

4½ cups, plus 2 tablespoons high-gluten flour

2⅓ cups whole wheat flour, preferably Maine grown and milled

5 teaspoons salt

1½ teaspoons dry yeast

The night before you plan to bake, prepare the poolish: In a large bowl, combine the 88°F water with the bread flour and dry yeast. Stir until combined. Let mixture rest, covered, in a warm spot, overnight, until it is ripe and has an acidic, sour scent.

To prepare the 7-grain cereal: In a medium-size saucepan over low heat, add the 7-grain mix to boiling water, cooking until it has thickened into a stiff porridge. Stir at 5 minute intervals to ensure that the bottom doesn't burn. Remove from heat. Cool to room temperature.

When you are ready to begin the bread, mix the poolish, the cooked 7-grain cereal, and the remaining ingredients in a stand mixer, using the dough hook attachment. Continue mixing until the dough is cohesive and just beginning to develop a bit of gluten.

Let the dough rest in a dough box, or covered in a warm spot, for 1 hour, and then give it a single stretch and fold. Let rest again for 1 hour. Turn out the dough onto a clean, floured surface. Divide into three pieces. Grease loaf pans and shape the dough into loaves. Let rise one more time, until dough is doubled in size. While the dough is rising, preheat oven to 425°F. Bake for 40 minutes, or until loaves sound hollow when rapped with a knuckle.

## CRAFT BREWS-BEER AND BEYOND

Maine brewers have been have been crafting artisan ales for decades, and their goods can be sampled on the Maine Beer Trail, a guided map of the best brewpubs and microbreweries around the state (*mainebrewersguild.org*). In the past few years, another crop of brewers has sprouted up: mead makers and cider fermenters. Working with ingredients that are native to Maine, craft meads, hard ciders, and kombucha are making a splash on the culinary scene. Businesses like Maine Mead Works (51 Washington Avenue; 207-773-6323), the Urban Farm Fermentory (200 Anderson Street, Bay 4; 207-653-7406), and Root Wild Kombucha (135 Washington Avenue; 207-468-4554) are based in Portland's East End, and they are turning out tasty brews with a light fizz and little kick. Made from local honey and apples, both mead and cider are drier than you'd expect, making them a refreshing alternative to beer and wine. Look for them by the bottle and on menus around town, or better yet, take a tour of one of the fermentories and stop by the tasting room.

# HIGH ROLLER LOBSTER

104 Exchange Street
(207) 560-7351
*highrollerlobster.com*
Chef/Owners: Baxter Key and Andy Gerry

Started in 2015 as a food cart serving fresh Maine lobster and crab on grilled brioche rolls, High Roller's following soon demanded a brick-and-mortar space to get their fix year-round. Now patrons can head to the Old Port seven days a week to satisfy their craving for lobster and crab rolls, tacos and hamburgers piled high with picked lobster meat, and High Roller's signature fried "lobby pops"—skewered lobster tails, cornmeal battered and fried, served with sauces that range from charred pineapple mayo to curried ketchup. In a high-energy space with painted exposed brick, shiny red booths and tables, and glowing neon lobsters illuminating the walls, chef/owners Baxter Key and Andy Gerry play with their menu, offering changing specials and fun happy hour pairings with local breweries. For those nostalgic for the original cart, High Roller offers catering.

For the recipes included here, using freshly cooked, just-picked lobster meat is essential. High Roller's Lobster Grilled Cheese sandwich is simple in concept but is somehow greater than the sum of its parts. Adjust the proportions of cheese to suit your preference. If the brands specified are unavailable in your area, substitute your favorite high-quality Swiss and extra-sharp cheddar cheeses.

Unlike many bisques, High Roller's is thickened with a puree of butternut squash, which imparts an earthy sweetness and makes it gluten free.

## LOBSTER GRILLED CHEESE
(MAKES 1 SERVING)

Jarlsberg Swiss cheese

Sharp cheddar cheese (such as Cabot Seriously Sharp Cheddar)

2 tablespoons unsalted butter, softened

2 slices English muffin bread, preferably from Portland's Big Sky Bakery

¼ pound cooked, shucked lobster meat

Cooked sliced bacon, optional

Avocado slices, optional

On the coarse side of a box grater, grate equal parts Jarlsberg and cheddar cheese. Set aside.

Butter each side of the bread. In a flat-bottomed, oven-safe skillet over medium-low heat, toast buttered bread low and slow until it's golden. Sprinkle cheese blend over one side of each slice of toasted bread, covering completely. Place under a broiler until cheese is completely melted.

Pull bread from broiler and spread lobster meat over the melted cheese. (At this point, you can also add toppings such as bacon or avocado.) Close the sandwich. Return skillet to medium-low and heat the sandwich to warm the lobster and give the bread a final crisp, about 1 minute each side. Cut on a diagonal and serve immediately.

# LOBSTER BISQUE

(MAKES 6 SERVINGS)

½ cup (1 stick) unsalted butter

1 large yellow onion, diced

1 large butternut squash, peeled and cut into large chunks

2 cups bottled clam juice

2 cups cream sherry

2 cups whipping cream

1 pound cooked, shucked lobster meat

Salt, to taste

Chopped parsley, to taste

Fresh thyme leaves, to taste

In a large pot over medium heat, melt butter. Add diced onion and cook until soft and translucent. Add squash and clam juice, cooking until squash is soft, about 30 minutes. Add sherry and then raise temperature to medium-high, bringing to a boil until the alcohol cooks off. Remove pot from heat.

Working in batches, process soup in a blender or food processor until it is smooth. (Alternatively, use an immersion blender to puree the soup in the pot.)

Return soup to pot and add whipping cream and lobster meat. Stir to incorporate, then season to taste with salt, chopped parsley, and fresh thyme leaves. Serve hot.

# IZAKAYA MINATO

54 Washington Avenue
(207) 613-9939
*izakayaminato.com*
Chef/Owner: Thomas Takashi Cooke
Co-Owner: Elaine Alden

In Japan an *izakaya* is a casual pub where patrons go for a drink and a snack—the word translates literally as "stay, sake, shop." At the bustling Izakaya Minato (*minato* translates to "harbor"), chef/owner Thomas Takashi Cooke brings this lesser-known Japanese eatery to Maine. The wait for a table on a weekend night demonstrates how the city has embraced *izakaya* dining. As an early enthusiastic headline from a review in *Maine Today* put it, this is "the Japanese gastropub Portland didn't even know it was dying for."

In a space dominated by an open kitchen and festooned with red lanterns (a decoration traditional to *izakayas* in Japan), diners choose from a menu of Japanese classics made with Maine's seasonal ingredients: locally foraged mushrooms, seasonal vegetables, and a changing daily sashimi appear alongside udon, *okonomiyaki,* and JFC (Japanese Fried Chicken). Bottled Japanese beers and a wide variety of Japanese whiskeys are available, with local Maine beers on tap, at the bar. Shareable carafes of sake can be sipped from antique sake cups, or ones made by Chef Cooke.

A proper dashi broth is at the foundation of Japanese cooking. Chef Cooke emphasizes the need to simmer the broth at a very low heat, paying close attention to it, to avoid releasing undesirable amino acids in the kombu and bonito flakes. You may want to keep a kitchen thermometer handy the first few times you make dashi to ensure that you stay in the range. Ingredients such as kombu, bonito flakes, and *shichimi togarashi* can be found in the Asian section of most grocery stores, or online.

# DASHI

(MAKES 3½–4 QUARTS)

4 quarts cold water

1 6-inch-long piece kombu (dried sea kelp)

Handful of *katsuo bushi* (dried bonito flakes)

In a large, heavy-bottomed pot, place cold water and kombu over very low heat. Slowly bring temperature to 185°F to 195°F, making sure that you do not bring it to a boil; boiling kombu will release amino acids that change the flavor of the broth. When water comes to this temperature (which will take 45 to 60 minutes), remove kombu from pot.

Add a large handful of *katsuo bushi* (dried bonito flakes) and 1 cup of cold water to the pot and turn heat up to high. As the water heats, small bubbles will form just before it comes to a boil (sometimes called "brightening"). Again, do not let the water come to a boil, as it will release undesirable flavors and will cloud the dashi. Within several minutes of turning the heat to high, the broth will return to 185°F to 195°F. Turn off the heat and let broth sit in the pot for 10 minutes.

Strain dashi through a cheesecloth-lined colander set in another large pot, letting the broth drain naturally without squeezing the cloth.

## Using the Dashi

Dashi is the foundation of many classic Japanese broths, such as the two soups here, which are served with cooked soba (buckwheat) noodles.

# HOT SOBA BROTH

(MAKES 4 SERVINGS)

1 quart dashi

1/4 cup soy sauce

¼ cup mirin

1 teaspoon salt

Combine all ingredients in a pot and bring to a simmer. This will be a somewhat lightly seasoned soup; add more soy sauce and salt as desired. Serve with cooked soba noodles.

# COLD SOBA DIPPING BROTH

(MAKES 4 SERVINGS)

1 quart dashi

½ cup soy sauce

½ cup mirin

1 teaspoon salt

Combine all ingredients in a pot and bring to a simmer. Remove from heat and chill until ready to use. Serve with cooked Soba noodles.

# SHIROMI ANKAKE (WHITEFISH TOPPED WITH SAUCE)

## (MAKES 3 OR 4 SERVINGS)

¼–½ cup mixed mushrooms (combination of shiitake, oyster, brown beech, and enoki), thinly sliced

1½ cups hot soba broth

1 tablespoon potato starch

2 tablespoons water

3–4 ounces cod, hake, or other firm-fleshed white fish, cut into 3 or 4 pieces

½ cup potato starch (cornstarch can substitute), or enough to coat the hake

Canola oil for frying

1 tablespoon grated daikon radish

½ teaspoon thinly sliced scallions

*Shichimi togarashi* (Japanese 7 spice blend), for serving (optional)

In a medium-size saucepan, place the mixed mushrooms in the hot soba broth to cook. In a small bowl, combine tablespoon of the potato starch with water and stir until smooth. Once the mushrooms are cooked and tender, thicken the broth with the potato starch mixture, stirring vigorously to prevent sauce from clumping.

Place remaining potato starch in a bowl and toss fish to coat. Heat 1½ inches of canola oil in a deep, straight-sided frying pan. When oil is hot, add fish and fry until crispy and lightly browned.

To serve, place cooked fish on a plate and pour on mushroom sauce. Top with grated daikon, sliced scallions, and a sprinkle of *shichimi togarashi*, if desired. Serve immediately.

# LB KITCHEN

249 Congress Street
(207) 775-2695
*lbkitchenportlandme.com*
Chef/Owner: Lee Farrington
Co-Owner: Bryna Gootkind

In an airy space at the base of Munjoy Hill, LB Kitchen serves up a delicious range of progressive, health-promoting foods. Steaming bowls of bone broth, golden wellness lattes, colorful grain bowls, and breakfast salads as composed as mosaics pack the menu in a fast-casual environment. Patrons grab something to go from the counter, perch on a cheery yellow stool, and watch the passersby on Congress Street from long communal tables while sipping a rainbow of vibrant smoothies and nibbling on avocado toast topped with leafy arugula.

Chef Lee Farrington, formerly of Figa, and her life and business partner, Bryna Gootkind, conceived the restaurant as a way to bring together their individual backgrounds in cooking and nutrition. Their collaboration is a welcome blend: nourishing foods that are both flavorful and fun. The restaurant has struck a chord in Portland, and the couple are in the process of opening a second location as the cafe in a wellness center on the opposite side of town.

At LB Kitchen, the kitchen keeps a smoked pepper spice blend on hand to liven up a variety of dishes, including the popular Avocado Addiction. The spice blend is a mix of smoked paprika, garlic powder, dried basil, and ground black pepper. Chef Farrington recommends experimenting with proportions according to your taste.

Heiwa tofu, used in the Tofu Banh Mi Bowl, is a local favorite made in Rockport, Maine. If it's not available in your area, substitute any firm tofu. LB Kitchen ferments their pickles and kimchi in house; use your preferred brand. Just Mayo vegan mayonnaise is used in the Sriracha Mayo, but any mayonnaise can be substituted.

# AVOCADO ADDICTION

(MAKES 1 SERVING)

½ avocado, pittted and seeded

¼ teaspoon smoked sea salt, like Maldon

½ teaspoon smoked pepper spice blend

⅛ teaspoon white truffle oil

¼ cup arugula leaves

1 teaspoon sherry vinegar

1 teaspoon olive oil

Salt and pepper, to taste

Sourdough bread, sliced to 1½-inch thickness

In a small mixing bowl, smash the avocado, leaving some chunks, and season with smoked sea salt, smoked pepper spice blend, and truffle oil.

In a separate small bowl, toss the arugula with the sherry vinegar, olive oil, and salt and pepper.

Toast the bread slices, and arrange on a plate. Mound the avocado mash on the toast, and top with the dressed arugula. Serve immediately.

---

# TOFU BANH MI BOWL

(MAKES 4 SERVINGS)

Secret Tofu Marinade (see recipe below)

Miso Sesame Slaw (see recipe below)

Sriracha Vegan Mayo (see recipe below)

Rice (see recipe below)

## Secret Tofu Marinade

¼ cup sriracha hot sauce

1 tablespoon sambal oelek chili paste

½ cup sugar

1 cup water

1 pound Heiwa tofu

Canola oil, for sautéing

**To make the tofu marinade:** Place sriracha, sambal oelek, sugar, and water in a small saucepan over low heat and whisk to combine. Warm, continuing to stir, until the sugar is dissolved. Set aside to cool.

Strain the tofu in a colander for about 15 minutes, then pat dry with a paper towel. Cut tofu into small cubes. Place cubed tofu in a small bowl and toss with the marinade. Refrigerate and let marinate for 2 to 6 hours, to absorb flavor. Before serving, drain tofu, reserving marinade for serving. Heat canola oil in a medium-size skillet over medium-high heat, and sauté tofu until edges are lightly browned.

## Miso Sesame Slaw

1 small head red cabbage, shredded

½ cup rice wine vinegar, divided

¼ cup sesame oil

½ cup white miso paste

Salt and pepper, to taste

**To make Miso Sesame Slaw:** In a large bowl, toss shredded cabbage with half the rice wine vinegar. In a separate small bowl, whisk together the remaining rice wine vinegar and the sesame oil and white miso paste. Dress the cabbage, toss, and taste to adjust seasonings.

## Sriracha Vegan Mayo

1 jar Just Mayo vegan mayonnaise

¼–½ cup sriracha sauce

**To make Sriracha Vegan Mayo:** In a medium-size bowl, whisk together the mayonnaise with sriracha sauce, according to taste. This mayo can be kept, covered, for up to 2 weeks in the refrigerator.

## Rice

1¾ cups water

¼ teaspoon salt

1 cup brown rice

**To make the rice:** In a medium-size saucepan over medium-high heat, bring water to a boil. Season with salt. Add the brown rice, and lower temperature to a simmer. Cover and cook for 45 to 50 minutes, until water is absorbed and rice is toothsome.

## The Dish

Hemp seeds, for serving

Sea salt, for serving

Salad greens, tossed with olive oil, sea salt, and sherry vinegar or lemon juice, if desired

½ cup kimchee, store bought or homemade

Pickled vegetables, store bought or homemade

**To compose each bowl:** In a large soup bowl, place several spoonfuls of rice. Toss with hemp seeds, sea salt, and a spoonful of reserved marinade. Using the back of a spoon, smear some Sriracha Mayo on the side of the bowl. In a separate small bowl, toss the sautéed tofu with some of the Sriracha Mayo and place on top of the rice. If desired, add dressed salad greens. Spoon Miso Sesame Slaw on top, and garnish with kimchee and pickled vegetables, if desired.

# LITTLE GIANT

Restaurant:
211 Danforth Street
Market:
81 Clark Street
(207) 747-5045
*littlegiantmaine.com*
Co-Owners: Andrew and Briana Volk
Chef: Neil Ross

With an exhortation to "Eat up, Bub," this second project from Andrew and Briana Volk, owners of the acclaimed Portland Hunt and Alpine Club (page 141), is a casual and welcoming restaurant, bar, and corner store in the residential West End neighborhood. In an open, well-lighted space, decorated with paintings based on the owners' family photos, solicitous servers recommend wine pairings and guide patrons through a menu that is both comforting and unexpected. Chef Neil Ross has brought a deep love of local ingredients—farmed, foraged, and made in Maine—to his creations. Pork belly is braised in Moxie soda, the "chips" served with cod swap cauliflower for the traditional potato. The Champagne and Lobster Chips, crisp and ethereal, defy description: On the menu they're simply paired with a quote from Dorothy Parker. The bar features a wide variety of wines and spirits, and cocktail offerings that merited inclusion in *GQ*'s list of America's Best New Bar Programs in 2018. In the attached market, the shelves are stocked with products from local purveyors—including such pantry staples as milk and eggs—as well as sandwiches and meals to go, a well-curated selection of wines, and a few choice culinary magazines and books, including the owners' own *Northern Hospitality*.

Mojo Picon is a traditional Spanish condiment. Any leftover sauce pairs beautifully with potatoes or with grilled meats. For the Blue Cheese Sauce, Queso de Valdeón is a Spanish blue cheese, traditionally made with cow's milk and wrapped in sycamore or chestnut leaves while it ages. If Valdeón is not available, substitute any bracing blue. Matsutake mushrooms are meaty and complex and are used ceremonially in Japan. They are foraged in Maine, where they grow beneath evergreens and are sometimes referred to as a "pine mushroom." Spruce sprigs can also be found in the woods of Maine, and their culinary use adds a wintry touch to dishes such as Little Giant's Beef Tenderloin with Uni Butter, Matsutake Mushrooms, Littleneck Clams, and Smoked Spruce and cocktails such as Blyth and Burrows' Ship, Captain, Crew.

# CABBAGE WITH WHIPPED HALIBUT AND CELERY ROOT PUREE

The recipe for Whipped Halibut and Celery Root Puree begins with curing a fillet of halibut for five days. This is a dish where planning ahead is essential! To ensure that all pieces of this creation are ready at the time of serving, it is best to begin by curing the halibut and making the Confit Garlic in advance. The day of serving, make the Whipped Halibut and Celery Root Puree and the Crispy Shallots before roasting the cabbage and assembling the dish.

(MAKES 4 SERVINGS)

½ cup grape seed oil

1 green cabbage, cut into quarters with core intact

4 tablespoons cider vinegar

4 cups Whipped Halibut and Celery Root Puree (see recipe below)

8 tablespoons Crispy Shallots (see recipe below)

Chili oil, to taste

Fresh dill sprigs

Sea salt, to taste

Preheat oven to 350°F.

In a large, cast iron pan over medium heat, heat the grape seed oil. Add the cabbage quarters, cut side down, and sauté until the leaves begin to brown and caramelize. Using tongs, flip each quarter over and saute on the other side. Turn cabbage so that its "back" is on the pan, and caramelize the outer leaves.

Return the cabbage quarters to their sides and place the pan in the oven, cooking until cabbage is soft, about 5 minutes. Remove pan from oven and pour in the cider vinegar, deglazing the pan and scraping up any browned bits with a wooden spoon. Set aside.

To assemble the dish: On each serving dish, place 1 cup of the Whipped Halibut and Celery Root Puree. Set the cabbage on top, cut side down. Season with sea salt, and garnish top with Crispy Shallots and chili oil and fresh dill to taste.

## Whipped Halibut and Celery Root Puree

(MAKES 4 SERVINGS)

1 pound celery root, peeled, trimmed, and diced

1 gallon whole milk

2 bay leaves

2 pieces dried cayenne pepper

1 pound Cured Halibut (see recipe below)

4 cloves Confit Garlic (see recipe below)

1 cup olive oil

Sea salt (to taste)

In a medium-size pot over medium-high heat, combine celery root, milk, bay leaves, and cayenne pepper pieces. Bring mixture to a boil, then reduce heat to medium-low to keep mixture at a simmer. Cook until the celery root is soft enough to pierce easily with a fork. Using a slotted spoon, scoop out the cooked celery root, and place in a large bowl.

Add the cured halibut to the milk mixture, and cook on medium-low heat until the fish begins to flake. Strain out the fish, placing it into the bowl with the celery root. Discard the milk mixture.

Using a stiff wire whisk, blend together the celery root and halibut. Fold in the confit garlic and the olive oil, and whip until the mixture is creamy. Adjust seasonings to taste, cover, and set aside until ready to assemble the dish.

## Cured Halibut

(MAKES 4 SERVINGS)

1 pound of filleted halibut, cleaned

½ cup plus 1 teaspoon salt

¼ cup sugar

7 whole garlic cloves, peeled and smashed (20 grams, by weight)

2 bay leaves

Thyme sprig

With a paper towel, pat dry the halibut. In a medium-sized nonreactive bowl, combine salt, sugar, garlic cloves, bay leaves, and thyme sprig. Spread half the cured mixture on a plate, place the halibut filet on top, and cover with remaining cure. Wrap in plastic and refrigerate for 5 days to let the fish cure. Rinse before using.

## Confit Garlic

(MAKES ½ CUP)

4 whole garlic cloves, peeled

½ cup grape seed oil

Combine garlic cloves and grape seed oil in a small saucepan. Cook over medium heat until the garlic is meltingly soft. Reserve until ready to use. Extra garlic-infused oil can be used in salad dressings and for imparting extra flavor to sautés.

## Crispy Shallots

(MAKES ¼ CUP)

2 clean shallots, peeled and trimmed

1 cup olive oil

Sea salt, to taste

On the thinnest setting of a mandoline, slice shallots. Place olive oil in a small pot and add shallots. Cook over medium heat until crispy and amber in color. Strain crispy shallots and set aside on a paper towel to remove excess oil. Season to taste with sea salt.

# BRUSSELS SPROUTS WITH MOJO PICON AND BLUE CHEESE SAUCE

(MAKES 4 SERVINGS)

1 pound Brussels sprouts, halved

Canola oil, for fryer

Sea salt, to taste

1 cup of Mojo Picon (see recipe below)

¼ pound Brussels sprouts leaves, separated into petals

¼ pound cilantro, picked (no stems)

¼ cup Lime Vinaigrette (see recipe below)

1 cup Blue Cheese Sauce (see recipe below)

Clean and pat dry halved Brussels sprouts. Fill fryer with canola oil and set temperature to 375°F. Working in batches, fry halved Brussels sprouts until they are crunchy and amber in color. Remove with a slotted spoon, and place in a large mixing bowl. When all the Brussels sprout halves have been fried, season with sea salt, to taste. Add the Mojo Picon to the mixing bowl, and toss to coat.

In a separate medium-size bowl, combine Brussels sprout leaves and picked cilantro leaves. Salt to taste, and add Lime Vinaigrette, tossing lightly to combine.

To serve, place a ¼ cup of Cheese Sauce at the base of each serving dish. Top with ¼ of the fried Brussels sprouts, and finish with ¼ of the fresh dressed Brussels sprouts and cilantro leaves.

## Mojo Picon

(MAKES 3 CUPS)

1 teaspoon ground cumin

1 teaspoon Spanish paprika (pimenton)

1 rounded tablespoon salt

1½ teaspoons dried habanero pepper

3 tablespoons ancho paste

10 whole garlic cloves, peeled

½ cup plus 3 tablespoons sherry vinegar

1 cup plus 2½ tablespoons blended oil

1 cup plus 2½ tablespoons olive oil

In a blender, combine cumin, pimenton, salt, vinegar, and dried habenero, and pulse to combine. Add ancho paste, whole garlic cloves, and sherry, and blend on high for 1 minute, until everything is fully incorporated. With the blender running, pour in the oils in a slow stream, blending until mixture is thickened. Set aside until ready to use.

## Lime Vinaigrette

(MAKES 2 CUPS)

⅔ cup lime juice

⅓ cup plus 2 tablespoons rice vinegar

1⅓ cups olive oil

1 teaspoon salt

Zest of two limes

Combine all ingredients in a blender, and mix on high until fully incorporated. Set aside until ready to use.

## Blue Cheese Sauce

(MAKES 1 QUART)

1.1 pounds (500 grams) blue cheese, preferably Queso de Valdeón

4 cups whole milk

Combine the blue cheese and the milk in a blender, and mix on high until thoroughly incorporated. Transfer to a nonreactive, heavy-bottomed sauce pan, and heat on low until sauce is just warmed and reaches 135 degrees. Set aside until ready to use.

## BEEF TENDERLOIN WITH UNI BUTTER, MATSUTAKE MUSHROOMS, LITTLENECK CLAMS, AND SMOKED SPRUCE

(MAKES 4 SERVINGS)

This dish contains several elements, all of which must be made before the steak. The Uni Butter and Garlic Puree can be made in advance, while the Matsutake Mushrooms and Littleneck Clams should be made right before the steak. It might go without saying, but the smoked sprig of spruce should be taken from a tree that has not been sprayed with pesticides. This dish takes a little extra effort but is well worth it!

1 cup Garlic Puree (see recipe below)

Beef Tenderloin (see recipe below)

Littleneck Clams (see recipe below)

Matsutake Mushrooms (see recipe below)

Reserved clam juice (with steak juices in it)

Olive oil

Sea salt

4 sprigs of spruce

In a small saucepan over low heat, warm the garlic puree. On a carving board, slice each steak against the grain.

To assemble the dish: at the base of each serving plate, spoon ¼ cup warmed garlic puree. Place 6 ounces of sliced steak and 4 clams on top of the puree on each dish. Divide the mushrooms evenly among the plates. Finish by spooning on the steak-infused clam juice, a dash or two of olive oil, and sea salt, to taste. Using a culinary torch or match, burn each spruce sprig so that it begins to smoke. Place smoking spruce on top of the steak and serve immediately.

## Garlic Puree

(MAKES 1 CUP)

20 cloves whole garlic, peeled and cleaned

1 quart (4 cups) cold water, separated

1 quart (4 cups) whole milk

2 tablespoons grape seed oil

Sea salt, to taste

In a medium-size saucepan, combine garlic cloves with 2 cups cold water. Bring to a boil over medium-high heat. Remove from heat and strain. Return garlic cloves to the pot with remaining 2 cups of cold water and bring to a boil again. Strain and return garlic to the pot. Add milk, reduce heat to medium, and bring mixture to the boil. Strain and discard milk.

Place cooked garlic into a blender and puree on high for 1 minute. Scrape down the sides to ensure that all the garlic is incorporated. With the blender running, add the grape seed oil to the pureed garlic in a slow stream, blending until smooth. Season to taste, and set aside until ready to use.

## Beef Tenderloin

(MAKES 4 SERVINGS)

4 6-ounce steaks, grass-fed beef tenderloin (as local as possible)

Sea salt, to taste

Olive oil

Thyme sprigs

8 cloves garlic, smashed

8 ounces Uni Butter (see recipe below)

Reserved clam juice

Preheat oven to 350°F. Pat dry the steak, and season with salt. Heat a cast iron pan over medium heat. Add enough olive oil to coat the pan, and heat until it shimmers but does not smoke. Add the tenderloin and sear on each side until there's a browned crust all around. Add the thyme sprigs, smashed garlic, and a dollop of uni butter to the top of each steak. Place the pan in the oven, and cook until a meat thermometer reads 120°F (steak will be rare). While steak is cooking, place reserved clam juice in a shallow dish.

Remove the steak from the cast iron pan and place the meat in the reserved clam juices. Let the steak rest in the juice for half the time it cooked (for example, if the steak is cooked for ten minutes, let it rest for five). Make sure to flip the steak over halfway through the resting time to ensure that the clam juices permeate the whole steak.

## Uni Butter

(MAKES 1 POUND)

1 pound cultured butter, at room temperature

¾ cup (200 grams) uni

Zest of 3 Meyer lemons

Place the butter in the top of a double boiler over simmering water. Let the butter heat and soften, whisking occasionally until it's thickened. Make sure that you don't overheat it, which will cause the butter to break.

Place the tempered butter in the bowl of a food processor with the uni and lemon zest. Blend on high until everything is thoroughly incorporated and whipped into a consistent uni-orange color. Set aside until ready to use.

## Littleneck Clams

(MAKES 4 SERVINGS)

16 littleneck clams

4 shallots, trimmed and sliced

8 cloves garlic, peeled and sliced

½ cup olive oil

1 cup white wine

Place clams in a large bowl of clean, fresh water. Let them sit in the water for 20 minutes. This will help the clams clean themselves—as they filter the fresh water, they will naturally push out any salt and sand that's collected in their shells. When ready to cook, remove them from the bowl and discard the water.

In a large, heavy-bottomed pot over medium heat, combine the shallots, garlic, and olive oil. Cook, stirring occasionally, until shallots are fragrant and translucent. Add the cleaned littleneck clams to the pot, and pour in the wine. Cover and cook until the clams open. Remove clams to a bowl, and reserve liquid. Set aside until ready to use.

## Matsutake Mushrooms

(MAKES 4 SERVINGS)

4–8 matsutake mushrooms

Olive oil

Thyme sprigs

4 cloves garlic, smashed

Using a paintbrush, clean the mushrooms without moistening, lightly brushing to loosen and remove any dirt or debris. Cut the mushrooms in half, lengthwise. On the flesh of the cut side, score the mushroom in a checkered or diamond pattern.

Heat a cast iron pan over medium heat. Add enough olive oil to coat the pan, and heat until it shimmers but does not smoke. Place mushrooms scored side down in the pan, and add the thyme sprigs and smashed garlic. Cook until the mushroom is lightly browned and the flesh is cooked through.

# LIQUID RIOT

250 Commercial Street
(207) 221-8889
*liquidriot.com*
Owner: Eric Michaud
Chef: Joshua Doria

Named in a nod to the 1855 Portland Rum Riots, which ended a four-year experiment in temperance that outlawed the production and sale of alcohol in the state of Maine, Liquid Riot is home to New England's only combination brewery, distillery, restaurant, and bar. Perched at the waterfront, the bustling resto-bar turns out well-crafted pub fare, from baskets of addictive fries with gochujang aioli to fish tacos and burgers, which earned it a spot as a featured brewery on the Travel Channel's *Food Paradise*. Liquid Riot's spirits, including Rum Riot Rum, Old Port Bourbon, and Fernet Michaud, a proprietary digestif named for the owners, have won awards from the American Distilling Institute, American Craft Spirits Association, and the New York World Wine and Spirits Competition.

Visible but off limits to diners are the shiny fermentation tanks and stills that support the brewery and distillery. Housing all of these under one roof underscores the mission to educate patrons on the crafts of small batch brewing and distilling. It has also led to some wonderful collaborations: A case in point is the "I Only Drink Beer" cocktail featured here, which combines Liquid Riot's Bierschnaps, a high-proof spirit traditionally made in Bavaria by distilling beer with a malt syrup and hop foam that riff on the brewery's main ingredients.

The recipes featured here use Liquid Riot's spirits, but if they are not available in your area, another fernet or bierschnaps may be substituted. Pilsen malt syrup is available online from brewing supply companies. Cream chargers, which use nitrous oxide to instantly whip cream and egg whites, are a common tool in commercial kitchens and can be ordered online. If you do not have one, you can whip the hops foam with a hand mixer, but it will break down and dissolve much more quickly.

# MUSHROOM TOAST

(MAKES 4 SERVINGS)

1 pound assorted mushrooms, preferably oyster and shiitake

2 tablespoons canola oil

4 sprigs fresh thyme

Salt and pepper, to taste

¼ cup bierschnaps

1 tablespoon sherry vinegar

Splash of mushroom stock or vegetable broth

2 tablespoons unsalted butter

4 slices sourdough bread

1 garlic clove, sliced horizontally

1 tablespoon extra virgin olive oil

Arugula and pickled red onions, for garnish (optional)

Clean and slice mushrooms into large pieces (they will shrink as they cook). Heat canola oil in a large saucepan over high heat, then sear mushrooms with the sprigs of thyme. Add salt and pepper to taste.

When mushrooms begin to turn golden, remove the thyme and deglaze the pan with bierschnaps. Light the spirits with a match and swirl, being careful of the flame. Once the fire has died down, add sherry vinegar, a splash of stock or broth, and the butter, stirring until the butter has melted.

Toast the sourdough and rub the warm bread with the cut side of the garlic. Generously drizzle toast with olive oil and salt and pepper to taste. Cut the sliced toast on a diagonal and pile on mushrooms. Spoon pan sauce over the top and serve, garnished with arugula and pickled red onions, if desired.

# FERNET MICHAUD ICE CREAM

## (MAKES 2 QUARTS)

3 cups, plus 3 tablespoons heavy cream

2⅓ cups whole milk

1 vanilla bean

6 sprigs fresh mint

8 egg yolks

1¼ cups granulated sugar

4 tablespoons milk powder

Pinch of salt

½ cup Fernet Michaud

In a large, heavy-bottomed saucepan over medium-high heat, bring heavy cream, whole milk, vanilla bean, and mint to a boil. Remove from heat. Let vanilla bean and mint sprigs steep.

In a large bowl, combine egg yolks, sugar, milk powder, and salt; whisk until thoroughly combined. Remove vanilla bean and mint sprig from the cream.

Whisking the egg mixture continuously, temper it by adding the hot cream mixture 1 cup at a time. Once you have added three quarters of the cream mixture, return the entire mixture to the pot and add the Fernet Michaud. Bring the mixture to 185°F, stirring continuously, and then remove from heat and place in an ice bath.

Once the mixture is chilled, place it in an airtight container and refrigerate overnight. Freeze following your ice cream maker's instructions, and let rest in a freezer for at least 4 hours before serving.

# "I ONLY DRINK BEER" COCKTAIL

### (MAKES 1 GENEROUS COCKTAIL)

2 ounces Liquid Riot Brewing Company
  Bierschnaps

1 ounce Toasted Pilsen Malt Syrup (see recipe
  below)

.75 ounce freshly squeezed lemon juice

3 ounces soda water

Hop Foam, for serving (see recipe below)

Combine the Bierschnaps, Toasted Pilsen Malt Syrup, and lemon juice in a highball glass. Fill with soda water and stir to combine. Top with Hop Foam before serving.

## Toasted Pilsen Malt Syrup

2¾ cups (600g) pilsen malt

3 cups (750g) water

4 cups (800g) sugar

In a medium-size pot, combine the sugar and water, and bring to a boil. Remove from heat and pour the hot liquid into a large, nonreactive container.

In a separate pan, lightly toast the pilsen malt for about 10 minutes, continually shaking the pan with the malt to keep it from burning. Add the hot, toasted malt to the hot syrup and stir. Let cool to room temperature, then strain before use.

## Hop Foam

1 cup water

1 cup egg whites

¼ cup heavy syrup (see note)

½ cup freshly squeezed lemon juice

8 drops hop extract

Note: To make heavy syrup, combine 2 parts sugar to 1 part water in a saucepan, and bring to a boil, stirring to dissolve the sugar. Cool to room temperature before use.

To make Hop Foam: To make the hop foam: In a 1 liter cream charger, combine all the ingredients. Refrigerate for 10 minutes. Charge once with nitrogen and shake the charger 12 times. Charge for a second time with nitrogen, and shake another 12 times. Keep foam refrigerated before use.

## SPIRITS

Passed in 1851, the Maine Liquor Law (also called The Maine Law), was America's first statewide temperance legislation. Left in place until the end of Prohibition in 1933, the law forbade distilling in the state, and led in 1855 to the Portland Rum Riot, after which Liquid Riot (page 93) is named. How times change! Maine is currently home to seventeen craft distillers, whose products include vodkas and gins made with Maine potatoes, bourbons from local corn, dark and light rums, and apple and blueberry brandies. Dotting the state, distilleries encourage visitors to drink locally made spirits, and they offer a wide range of small batch liquors to choose from. Botanicals like Chesuncook from Maine Craft Distilling (123 Washington Avenue; 207-699-4447)—made from a proprietary blend of carrot, juniper, mint, and coriander—celebrate the flavors from farm to flask. Stop by a tasting room, or visit the Maine Distillers Guild (mainedistillersguild.org) to find a map of the state's distilleries.

# Lolita Vinoteca + Asador

90 Congress Street
(207) 775-5652
*lolita-portland.com*
Chef/Owner: Guy Hernandez
Co-Owners: Stella Hernandez and Neil Reiter

Perched near the top of Munjoy Hill, Lolita Vinoteca + Asador is a cozy space, specifically designed to be a comfortable neighborhood hangout. Opened in 2014, the restaurant is the next evolution of Bar Lola, a fine dining restaurant previously owned and operated by Chef Guy Hernandez, his wife and general manager, Stella Hernandez, and their business partner Neil Reiter. Combining a *vinoteca* (wine cellar) with an *asador* (spit roast), Chef Hernandez modeled the restaurant on an Old World bodega—an open, welcoming space where "guests can stop in throughout the day for an espresso, a martini and a plate of olives, or a full dinner."

A visible wood-fired oven, in which everything from marrow bones to meaty carrots are roasted, separates the zinc bar that runs along one side of the restaurant from the bustling kitchen at the back. Serving a pan-Mediterranean collection of flavors that travel from Spain through North Africa and the Middle East, the menu is structured with a keen attention to foundations and accents, reflecting Hernandez's training as an architect. Above the tables, a remarkable selection of wines are on display, curated by Stella and taken down to pair with patrons' meals. Wines are the focus each Monday, when the restaurant offers a special tapas menu, with four wines centered on a theme—country, region, or grape varietal—paired with small plates from the kitchen.

The Grilled Quail with Chermoula and Couscous is a versatile dish—the couscous can be swapped for quinoa to make it gluten free; grilled chicken or a firm-fleshed fish can replace the quail; and extra chermoula sauce, a North African pantry staple, will keep for up to two weeks in the refrigerator. To toast spices, place them in a dry skillet over medium-high heat until they are fragrant. Grind them in a spice grinder, in a clean coffee grinder, or by hand with a mortar and pestle.

Making gnocchi by hand can be time-consuming, but they are well worth the effort. Chef Hernandez uses Maine's Lakin Gorges basket-drained ricotta, but any basket-drained ricotta can be substituted. Gnocchi freeze well for up to a month, if arranged in a single layer on parchment paper. Frozen gnocchi can be cooked directly from the freezer.

# GRILLED QUAIL WITH CHERMOULA AND COUSCOUS

## (MAKES 4 APPETIZER PORTIONS OR 2 SUBSTANTIAL PLATES)

### Chermoula

1 cup curly parsley, washed and roughly chopped

2 cloves garlic, peeled and crushed

1 teaspoon toasted cumin seeds, finely ground

1 teaspoon toasted coriander seeds, finely ground

1 teaspoon toasted caraway seeds, finely ground

1 cup olive oil

2 cups cilantro, washed and roughly chopped

Zest of 1 lemon

Salt and black pepper, to taste

**To make the chermoula:** In a blender or bowl of a food processor, puree the parsley, garlic cloves, and ground spices with ½ cup of the olive oil until smooth. Add cilantro and continue to process, slowly adding more olive oil until you have a smooth puree. Stir in lemon zest and season with salt and pepper.

### Couscous

1 cup dry couscous (not instant)

1 tablespoon kosher salt

1 cup warm water

2 tablespoons olive oil

**To prepare the couscous:** In medium-size bowl, season dry couscous with salt and cover with warm water. Set aside for 20 minutes to rehydrate. Add olive oil to reconstituted couscous and rub between your fingers to break up any clumps.

Line the basket of a steamer with a layer of cheesecloth to prevent couscous from falling through. Steam rehydrated couscous over salted water for 20 to 30 minutes, until soft and fluffy.

### Quail

4 semi-boneless quail

Olive oil

Salt and black pepper, to taste

Aleppo chile pepper, to taste

Zest of 1 lemon

**To prepare the quail:** Start a charcoal or wood fire. (Alternatively, you can use a gas grill or oven broiler.)

In a large bowl, toss quail with olive oil and season with salt, black pepper, aleppo chile pepper, and lemon zest.

When coals, grill, or broiler are ready, cook quail breast-side down for 4 to 6 minutes, rotating every couple of minutes, until skin is crispy. Using a large spatula, flip over the quail and cook another 6 to 8 minutes. The breast meat will still be a little pink. Set quail aside on a resting rack.

**To assemble the dish:** Fluff couscous with a fork and divide between four warmed plates. Top couscous with grilled quail and a spoonful of chermoula.

# RICOTTA GNOCCHI WITH ROASTED DELICATA SQUASH

## (MAKES 4 APPETIZER PORTIONS OR 2 MAIN COURSE SERVINGS)

4 tablespoons unsalted butter

1 cup walnut pieces, gently crushed

2 cups Roasted Delicata Squash (see recipe below)

12 ounces Ricotta Gnocchi (see recipe below)

Juice of ½ lemon

1 cup curly parsley, washed and roughly chopped

4 tablespoons freshly grated Parmesan cheese

### Roasted Delicata Squash

1 medium delicata squash (about ¾–1 pound)

Olive oil

Salt and black pepper

**To prepare the squash:** Preheat oven to 425°F and line a sheet pan with parchment paper. Wash outside of the squash but do not peel. Trim ends and cut in half lengthwise. Scoop out seeds, then cut in semicircles, about ¼- to ½-inch thick.

Toss squash with olive oil and season generously with salt and black pepper. Arrange in a single layer on the prepared sheet pan. Roast in the preheated oven for 15 minutes.

Rotate tray and roast another 12 minutes, until soft and golden.

### Gnocchi

1½ pounds basket-drained ricotta

2 eggs

Zest of 1 lemon

2 teaspoons kosher salt

2 cups all-purpose flour

**To make the gnocchi:** In a medium-size bowl, combine ricotta with eggs, lemon zest, and kosher salt, beating until well incorporated. Stir in flour and gently knead until dough comes together into a ball. Let dough rest 20 to 30 minutes.

To form the gnocchi, break off a handful of dough and roll it into a rope about the width of a thumb. Using a small paring knife or bench scraper, cut the rope into individual dumplings, roughly 1-inch long. Arrange gnocchi in single layer on a lightly floured, parchment-lined baking sheet. Cook according to the recipe below. If you do not use immediately, gnocchi can be frozen and stored for up to a month and cooked directly from the freezer.

**To make the dish:** Bring a large pot of salted water to a boil. Set a wide sauté or frying pan over medium-high heat. Add butter and crushed walnuts to pan and cook gently until butter starts to brown and nuts begin to toast. Add roasted squash to the pan; stir to coat with the butter and nuts. Remove from heat and set aside.

Drop gnocchi into boiling water and cook just until they begin to float to the surface. Scoop out with a slotted spoon.

With the heat off, add cooked gnocchi to the pan with brown butter, walnuts, and roasted squash. Toss with lemon juice and chopped parsley.

To serve, divide between warm bowls and top with grated Parmesan cheese.

# MaiZ

Public Market House
28 Monument Square, 2nd Floor
(207) 400-2881
*maizportland.com*
Chef/Owners: Martha Leonard and Niky Dwin Watler Amaris

Up the stairs of the Public Market House, under tall windows facing Monument Square, the griddle at Maiz turns out hundreds of *arepas* each day. This Colombian street food—a thick cornmeal cake stuffed with meats, cheeses, and vegetables and drizzled with creamy sauce—was a staple of their diets when American-born Martha Leonard met her husband, Niky Amaris, in Cartagena. Leonard eats gluten free, and she was amazed by how good she felt eating a diet of simple, whole foods while living in Colombia. Though neither partner have a background in the restaurant business—Leonard was a special education teacher and Amaris practiced law—the couple shared a dream of starting a business that would nourish "not only bodies, but also relationships and communities." The two have done just that, developing a strong following in Portland and beyond and receiving national recognition from, among others, the editors of *Bon Appetit*.

Traditionally, *arepas* are filled with slow-cooked pork, chorizo, and *queso blanco*, but Niky

notes that there is virtually no food that can't be served in an *arepa*! At Maiz, *arepas rellena* (filled *arepas*) are stuffed with both traditional fillings and some not so traditional, like vegan spiced cauliflower, and topped with a drizzle of *salsa rosada*. In lieu of *queso blanco*, Maiz substitutes a mixture of mozzarella and feta. On the side, have a cup of rich Colombian coffee or a local Green Bee soda.

The instructions below are for traditional *arepas*, made from cooked or frozen hominy, and for two variations made with *masa harina* (precooked ground cornmeal). *Choclo*, or Sweet Corn *Arepas*, are made from a special sweetened *harina* mix. At Maiz, the preferred brand is the South American staple P.A.N., which is available in most grocery stores and online. Salsa rosada, a traditional accompaniment, is a very simple but popular Colombian sauce. "Salsa" simply means sauce, and "rosada" describes its pink color.

## TRADITIONAL *AREPAS*

Cooked hominy corn

Salt, to taste

Canola oil

Note: For traditional *arepas*, cooked hominy can be either frozen precooked and then thawed, or dried and cooked according to package instructions.

After the hominy is cooked, squeeze out all the water by pressing it in a colander. Grind the hominy by pulsing in a food processor until it is a fine powder. Mix the ground hominy powder with salt, to taste, and enough canola oil to bind it together and make a soft dough.

Place the *arepa* dough into a medium-size bowl and mix with cheese or chopped vegetables, if desired. Using your hands, shape the dough into a thin patty and cook on an ungreased pan or griddle, 5 minutes each side. The *arepa* is ready when it lifts from the pan and can be flipped without sticking. Serve hot. *Arepas* can be split and stuffed with cheese, vegetables, or meat, or topped with additional cheese and/or *salsa rosada*.

# EVERYDAY WHITE CORN *AREPAS*

## (MAKES 4 SERVINGS)

1 cup *masa harina* (precooked white cornmeal)

1 teaspoon salt

1 cup water

In a medium-size bowl, mix together masa harina and salt. Slowly pour in the water, and mix together with your hands, massaging the dough until it is firm but pliable. Form balls to desired size and flatten them with your hands or a flat surface to form a thin disk. Cook on an ungreased pan or griddle, 5 minutes each side. The *arepa* is ready when it lifts from the pan and can be flipped without sticking. Serve hot. *Arepas* can be split and stuffed with cheese, vegetables, or meat, or topped with additional cheese and/or *salsa rosada*.

# *CHOCLO* (SWEET CORN *AREPAS*)

## (MAKES 4 SERVINGS)

1 cup *harina de choclo*

¾ cup water

⅓ cup milk

Unsalted butter

In a medium-size bowl, mix the *harina de choclo* (sweet corn flour) with the water and let it rest to settle and thicken. Mix in the milk, and let it rest again until it is the consistency of a thick pancake batter.

Generously butter a hot pan or griddle and pour the batter onto the pan to the desired size and shape. Cook until set, then flip and continue cooking until both sides are golden. Top with whatever you'd like and serve hot!

# SALSA ROSADA

## (MAKES 1½ CUPS)

1 cup mayonnaise

½ cup ketchup

1 teaspoon garlic powder

½ habanero pepper or other hot pepper

In the bowl of a food processor, combine all ingredients and pulse until well blended. This traditional Colombian sauce will keep well in the refrigerator for up to 2 weeks.

# Mami

339 Fore Street
(207) 536-4702
*mamifoodtruck.com*
Chef/Owner: Austin Miller
Co-Owner: Hana Tamaki

When Mami co-owner Hana Tamaki was five years old, she began learning to cook traditional Japanese dishes at the elbow of her father, one of Portland's first sushi chefs. Many years later, working at a restaurant with Chef Austin Miller, she made him a dish of *okonomiyaki*, a savory pancake, that transformed his cooking—and both their lives. That first taste of homey *izakaya*-style Japanese street food inspired in Miller an obsession with approachable Japanese cooking, and brought the two together as a couple. In 2015, Miller and Tamaki bought a food truck and found great success with their menu of steamed buns, Japanese-style hot dogs, skewered chicken, donburi rice bowls, and, of course, *okonomiyaki*. Two years later the couple opened a restaurant in the Old Port, serving expanded offerings in an open space dotted with intimate tables, comfortable sofas, and an L-shaped bar. Working with local farmers, foragers, and fishers, Chef Miller combines local ingredients with Japanese cooking techniques in dishes that have earned Mami national attention: The restaurant was named by *Bon Appetit* as one of the top twenty restaurants in Portland, and Chef Miller was featured on the Food Network's *Chopped*.

*Okonomiyaki* is a versatile dish that can be filled with whatever seasonal vegetables you have on hand. The bacon or pork belly can be swapped for another meat if you'd like—at Mami, a favorite substitute is octopus. The toppings can be found at most Asian markets. Dashi broth can be made from scratch (see Izakaya Minato, page 74), or can be purchased from concentrate at Asian and specialty markets.

# OKONOMIYAKI

(MAKES 4-6 SERVINGS)

2 cups dashi

1¼ cups all-purpose flour

2 eggs, lightly beaten

1 handful cabbage, thinly sliced

1 handful seasonal vegetables, blanched and sliced

¼ onion, julienned

Oil, for cooking

3–4 strips of bacon or pork belly, sliced

Okonomi sauce

Kewpie (Japanese mayonnaise)

Katsuobushi (smoked fish flakes)

Aonori (dried seaweed)

1 scallion, thinly sliced

Beni shoga (pickled ginger)

In a large bowl, mix dashi and flour until thoroughly combined. Beat in eggs until the batter is slightly thinner than traditional pancake batter, but not watery. Stir in cabbage, blanched seasonal vegetables, and onions; mix until combined.

Preheat a nonstick pan or a flat-top grill or griddle over medium-high heat. Place a few drops of oil on the pan, then pour in the *okonomiyaki* batter. Once the batter has begun to cook, add the bacon or pork belly. After 3 to 4 minutes, the searing side should be a light golden brown. Using a large spatula, flip the *okonomiyaki* and begin searing the uncooked side. Cook for 3 to 4 minutes more, then flip again and cook until crispy. Flip out of the pan, placing the *okonomiyaki* bacon-side down on a cutting board. Using a large knife or a pizza cutter, slice into sixths.

To serve, top with a generous amount of okonomi sauce and kewpie, and a sprinkle of katsuobushi, aonori, and thinly sliced scallions. Place a small handful of beni shoga in the center before serving.

# MR. TUNA

**Public Market House**
**28 Monument Square**
*mrtunamaine.com*
Chef/Owner: Jordan Rubin
Co-Owner: Marisa Lewiecki

Started in the summer of 2017 as a food cart off Commercial Street selling the "healthy street food" of hand rolls and sushi "burritos," Mr. Tuna's meteoric rise—legions of followers, a mention in *Bon Appetit*, and a brick-and-mortar sushi counter in the Public Market—is a testament to its novel combination of traditional sushi methods with abstract flavors and a playful streak. Chef Jordan Rubin, aka Mr. Tuna, has spent the better part of two decades honing his skills, working as a sashimi chef at Boston's Uni and a crudo chef at Portland's Solo Italiano (page 167) before striking out on his own. Working with raw seafood from different cultural angles has given him insight and flexibility into the possibilities of the daily catch. Freed from the hard-and-fast rules of classical sushi, Mr. Tuna experiments with flavors and form. The trick, he says, is to keep it simple while using fresh ingredients, homemade sauces, and the highest quality fish. This approach has earned him many admirers, who watch his Instagram eagerly to see where to find the cart each week of summer. As of October 2018, Mr. Tuna can be found year-round on the first floor of the Public Market House.

Mr. Tuna's space-age avocado ball, a popular appetizer, combines tuna tartare with creamy sliced avocado. Yellowtail or other sushi-grade fish can be substituted for the tuna, if desired. Homemade garlic ponzu sauce, a pungent twist on a Japanese staple, can be kept for up to two weeks in the refrigerator, and can be served with fish and grilled meats. Mr. Tuna makes his crispy shallots fresh for diners, but they can be found ready-made in most Asian markets.

# TUNA AVOCADO BALL WITH GARLIC PONZU

## (MAKES 2 SERVINGS)

Tuna Tartare (see recipe below)

1 avocado

Garlic Ponzu (see recipe below)

Crispy Shallots (see recipe below)

Fresh cilantro leaves

### Tuna Tartare

4 ounces sushi-grade tuna, finely chopped

2 tablespoons chives, finely chopped

Zest of ½ lemon

Flaky sea salt, to taste

**To make Tuna Tartare:** In a small bowl, combine all ingredients and mix well. Reserve, chilled, until ready to use.

### Garlic Ponzu

2 tablespoons freshly squeezed lime juice

1 clove garlic, peeled and pressed

2 tablespoons freshly squeezed lemon juice

2 tablespoons freshly squeezed orange juice

¼ cup soy sauce

1 tablespoon mirin (sweet Japanese rice wine)

**To make Garlic Ponzu:** In a small bowl, combine all ingredients and whisk until thoroughly incorporated. This sauce can be kept, covered, for up to 3 weeks in the refrigerator.

### Crispy Shallots

4 ounces shallots, peeled and thinly sliced

⅓ cup potato starch or cornstarch

Canola oil, for frying

Kosher salt, to taste

**To make Crispy Shallots:** In a deep skillet, bring canola oil to 325°F. Dust shallots in potato starch or cornstarch, lightly coating. Shake off excess starch and fry until golden brown. Remove shallots with a skimmer and place on a paper towel–covered sheet pan. Season with salt.

**To assemble the avocado ball:** Cut avocado in half lengthwise, separate halves, and remove pit and skin. Reserve one half.

Lay avocado cut-side down on a cutting board. Thinly slice avocado lengthwise, leaving slices next to each other.

Tear a 10-inch piece of plastic wrap and spread onto cutting board. Place avocado flat-side up (so that the hollow left by the removed pit is facing up) in the center of the plastic wrap. Fan out avocado slices in a circle on the plastic wrap. Mound half the tartare mixture in the center. Pull all sides of the plastic wrap together to form a ball, twisting until it is tight. Gently remove plastic wrap.

Repeat with the other half of the avocado and the rest of the tartare mixture.

To serve, place each avocado ball in the center of a shallow bowl and pour Ponzu Sauce around it. Top with Crispy Shallots and garnish with fresh cilantro leaves.

# NOBLE BARBECUE

1706 Forest Avenue
(207) 536-1395
*noblemeats.com*
Owner: Ryan Carey
Chefs: Paul Baldacci and Ryan LaMunyon

Venture to this casual barbecue spot, and you may be surprised by the steady stream of diners making their way to a residential stretch of outer Forest Avenue. The line at the counter begins in late morning, when daily specials written on brown butcher paper are pinned to the mustard-yellow walls. By noon it's hard to find a seat at the wooden tables, topped with house-made red and yellow barbecue sauces labeled with Noble's distinctive argyle-diamond logo. Outside, the "mobile Noble" food truck—the origin of the restaurant—is parked with its tableau of animals at a banquet facing the restaurant's windows.

Opened in 2017 as a home base and year-round outpost of owner Ryan Carey's catering business, Fire and Company, Noble Barbecue is both a restaurant in its own right and the staging ground for the catering side, with a staff who works on both sides of the business. Carey notes that his staff was the inspiration for the business: They work so well together that he started the restaurant to keep his team through the winter. Coming from fine-dining backgrounds, chefs Paul

Baldacci and Ryan LaMunyon bring to the kitchen a keen attention to detail: Fried chicken sandwiches come on a brioche bun, meatloaf is smeared with a long-simmered bacon jam, and vegetable garnishes are pickled in-house.

Surprisingly for a barbecue joint, the Smoked Spaghetti Squash Sandwich is one of several completely vegetarian offerings on the menu. Each sandwich is composed of several components, which are versatile and can be used to liven up other dishes. Try Tomato Jam on grilled cheese, or Bacon Jam as a base for its own sandwich. Noble's Smoky Chipotle Barbecue sauce is perfect with fried chicken, but for meat or squash that has also been smoked, use your favorite bottled barbecue sauce. Note: The spaghetti squash and meatloaf recipes featured here require a smoker to achieve the complex flavors they bring to each sandwich.

## SMOKED SPAGHETTI SQUASH SANDWICH
### (MAKES 8 SERVINGS)

Smoked spaghetti squash

Canola oil

Salt and pepper

Barbecue sauce, to taste

Tomato Jam (see recipe below)

Pimiento Cheese (see recipe below)

Fried Bread-and-Butter Pickles (see recipe below)

Shredded red cabbage

8 brioche buns, toasted and buttered

**To smoke the spaghetti squash:** Cut spaghetti squash in half lengthwise. Scoop out seeds and membrane. Coat with canola oil and season generously with salt and pepper. Smoke at 220°F for 3 hours. Shred with a fork (discarding the outer shell) and coat with your favorite barbecue sauce.

Tomato Jam

½ Vidalia onion, cut into small dice

1 teaspoon canola oil

1½ teaspoons ground cumin

1½ teaspoons kosher salt

1 teaspoon red pepper flakes

2 cinnamon sticks

¼ teaspoon ground cloves

½ teaspoon ground ginger

1½ teaspoons allspice

3 (20-ounce) cans chopped tomatoes

1 cup golden raisins

2 cups brown sugar

2 lemons, zested and juiced

**To make Tomato Jam:** In a large, heavy-bottomed pot, cook onion with oil until translucent. Add spices and toast mixture for 1 minute. Add tomatoes, raisins, and brown sugar. Cook on low until thick, stirring occasionally, about 2 hours. Remove from heat, remove cinnamon sticks, and stir in lemon zest and juice. Tomato jam will keep refrigerated in an airtight container for 2 weeks.

## Pimiento Cheese

1½ pounds cream cheese

1½ cups finely chopped pimiento

1 cup shredded cheddar cheese

½ cup mayo

¾ teaspoon garlic powder

¾ teaspoon onion powder

Salt to taste

**To make Pimiento Cheese:** Combine all ingredients in the bowl of a stand mixer. Use the paddle attachment to thoroughly combine.

## Fried Bread-and-Butter Pickles

Bread-and-butter pickles, sliced and drained

Flour for dredging

Canola oil, for frying

**To make Bread-and-Butter Pickles:** Toss pickles in a bowl of flour until they are lightly coated. In a deep fryer, or a deep, straight-sided frying pan filled with 2 inches of oil, fry pickles until crisp.

**To assemble the sandwich:** Place smoked and sauced spaghetti squash on toasted brioche buns with dollops of Tomato Jam, Pimiento Cheese, red cabbage, and Fried Bread-and-Butter Pickles.

# SMOKED MEATLOAF CHEESEBURGER

(MAKES 8 SERVINGS)

Smoked Meatloaf (see recipe below)

Bacon Jam (see recipe below)

8 slices cheddar cheese

Caramelized onions

Bread-and-butter pickles, sliced

Ketchup

8 brioche buns, toasted and buttered

## Smoked Meatloaf

2 pounds ground beef

4 tablespoons salt

1 tablespoon black pepper

Pinch of red pepper flakes

½ cup heavy cream

1 egg

1 teaspoon liquid smoke

1 teaspoon Worcestershire sauce

1 teaspoon apple cider vinegar

2 teaspoons molasses

½ cup crushed crackers (such as Ritz)

¼ cup brown sugar

1 teaspoon paprika

1 teaspoon ground cumin

2 teaspoons garlic powder

Barbecue sauce, to taste

**To make Smoked Meatloaf:** In a large bowl, mix the beef with salt, pepper, and red pepper flakes. In separate medium-size bowl, whisk together the wet ingredients, then stir in the cracker crumbs, brown sugar, and spices. Add the cracker mixture to the meat, and bring everything together, kneading with your hands to make sure it's mixed thoroughly. Form into a loaf and place into a meatloaf or metal bread pan. Top with barbecue sauce. Cook in a smoker at 220°F for 3½ hours, or until the internal temperature reads 150°F and the juices run clear.

Bacon Jam

1½ pounds bacon, chopped

6 yellow onions, julienned

¼ cup balsamic vinegar

2 cups maple syrup

4 cups brown sugar

½ cup whole grain mustard

1 bay leaf

Salt and pepper, to taste

**To make Bacon Jam:** In a large skillet over medium-high heat, cook chopped bacon until crisp. Remove bacon from pan, reserving 1 tablespoon of the fat.

In a separate, heavy-bottomed pot, sauté onions in reserved bacon fat until they start to brown. Deglaze the pan with balsamic vinegar, then turn the heat down to a low simmer. Add remaining ingredients and cook, stirring often, until mixture is thickened. Remove bay leaf before serving.

**To assemble the sandwich:** Slice the meatloaf into 8 (roughly ⅓-inch) slabs. Heat a griddle or cast iron skillet and sear meatloaf slices on each side. Top each slice with cheddar cheese, and allow to melt. Serve on toasted brioche buns with Bacon Jam, a dollop of ketchup, and a generous scattering of caramelized onions and bread-and-butter pickles.

## NOBLE MAC 'N' CHEESE

### (MAKES 12 SERVINGS)

1 cup melted butter

1 cup all-purpose flour

2 quarts whole milk

2 teaspoons garlic powder

2 teaspoons onion powder

1 teaspoon smoked paprika

2 tablespoons kosher salt

4 cups shredded yellow cheddar cheese

1 cup Pimiento Cheese (see page 119)

6 cups cooked macaroni

Crushed crackers (such as Ritz), for garnish

Scallions, sliced, for garnish

In a large, heavy-bottomed pot over low heat, whisk together the melted butter and flour to form a roux. Cook, stirring continuously, for about 5 minutes to cook out the flour taste. Slowly add milk, whisking often to avoid lumps. Stir in the spices. When all the milk is incorporated and the mixture is hot, whisk in the cheeses. Continue whisking until the sauce is smooth, then fold in the cooked macaroni. Serve hot, garnished with crushed crackers and scallions.

# NOBLE FRIED CHICKEN

## (MAKES 4-6 SERVINGS)

2 pounds boneless, skinless chicken thighs, trimmed and butterflied

Brine (see recipe below)

### Brine

½ cup salt

¼ cup sugar

8 cups hot water

Noble Chicken Coating (see recipe below)

1 quart buttermilk

Canola oil, for frying

2 tablespoons toasted fennel seed

2 tablespoons toasted black peppercorn

4 bay leaves

6 raw garlic cloves

**To make the brine:** Whisk together brine ingredients in a nonreactive container and chill.

### Noble Chicken Coating

4 cups all-purpose flour

4 cups semolina flour

½ cup onion powder

½ cup onion powder

½ cup crushed black pepper

**To make the Noble Chicken Coating:** In a large, bowl, combine ingredients, mixing thoroughly.

**To make the chicken:** Place the chicken thighs in a large, nonreactive bowl. Pour the brine over the chicken and allow to set in the refrigerator for at least 12 hours.

Drain brine from the bowl and pour the buttermilk over the chicken. Allow chicken to rest in the buttermilk for at least an hour.

Working in batches, pull chicken thighs from buttermilk and dredge in coating. In a deep fryer or large skillet, fry chicken in canola oil at 350°F until internal temperature reads 150°F.

# NOBLE CHICKEN "BANGER" SANDWICH

### (MAKES 6 SANDWICHES)

Noble Fried Chicken (see recipe above)

Chipotle Barbecue Sauce (see recipe below)

Ranch Coleslaw (see recipe below)

Sour dill pickles, sliced

6 brioche buns, toasted and buttered

## Chipotle Barbecue Sauce

1 small can (7 ounce) chipotle peppers in adobo sauce

4 cups apple cider vinegar

4 cups ketchup

2 cups brown sugar

1 cup honey

3 tablespoons onion powder

3 tablespoons garlic powder

½ tablespoon celery seed

2 tablespoons kosher salt

1 tablespoon black pepper

To make Chipotle Barbecue Sauce: Using a blender, puree the chipotle peppers with 2 cups of the vinegar. In a large, heavy-bottomed pot over low heat, combine chipotle puree with remaining 2 cups of vinegar and all ingredients and bring to a simmer, stirring regularly. Cook until flavors have blended and sauce is slightly reduced and thickened. When stored in an airtight container, this versatile barbecue sauce will keep for up to a month in the refrigerator.

## Ranch Coleslaw

4 cups mayonnaise

½ cup buttermilk

4 cloves garlic, minced or pressed

1 shallot, minced

2 teaspoons dried chives

2 teaspoons dried parsley

1 teaspoon dried dill weed

Salt and pepper, to taste

1 head green cabbage, sliced thin

1 carrot, julienned

Salt and pepper, to taste

To make Ranch Coleslaw: In the bowl of a food processor, combine the mayonnaise, buttermilk, garlic, shallot, and spices; pulse until smooth.

In a large bowl, toss together the cabbage and carrots. Mix dressing with the vegetables and serve immediately.

To assemble the sandwiches: Scoop a dollop of Chipotle Barbecue Sauce in a bowl and roll the fried chicken around to lightly coat with sauce. Place chicken on a toasted brioche bun, and top with sour dill pickles and Ranch Coleslaw.

## TAKING FARM-TO-TABLE A FEW STEPS FURTHER

As the farm-to-table restaurant movement gains momentum around the country, Maine's chefs are taking things a step further. Longtime proponents of local ingredients—Portland's acclaimed Chef Sam Hayward, James Beard's 2004 Best Chef in the Northeast, has been naming the provenance of meats and vegetables on his menu for decades—many chefs are now beginning to cultivate their own. On small farms that ring Portland's metro area, chefs work with farms in winter to ensure that they'll have the ingredients they need during Maine's growing season. Some, like Chef Josh Berry at Union (page 207) have gone a step further, keeping bees on his downtown rooftop for the restaurant's honey. Chef Cara Stadler—of Portland's Bao Bao Dumpling House and Lio and Brunswick's Tau Yuan—has built a rooftop aquaponic greenhouse to supply her restaurants. While he doesn't raise the animals, Pete Sueltenfuss of the Other Side Delicatessen (page 127) goes "whole hog," buying entire animals to butcher and cure himself. At the annual Pigs and Pinks fundraiser for Full Plates, Full Potential, an organization dedicated to fighting hunger in Maine, more than a dozen chefs work "nose to tail," using every part of two locally raised pigs for a meaty feast. With creativity and passion, many of Portland's best chefs work within the state's short northern growing season, embracing Maine's agricultural heritage and bringing its unique flavors to the table.

# OTHER SIDE DELICATESSEN

164 Veranda Street
(207) 761-9650
and
235 Vaughan Street
(207) 874-7414
*othersidedeli.com*
Chef/Owner: Pete Sueltenfuss

A butcher's apron may seem a far cry from a white chef's coat, but for Chef Pete Sueltenfuss, the transition was a natural one. After more than a decade in the restaurant business—culminating with a spell as the executive chef at Portland's Grace—Sueltenfuss decided to pursue his passion for charcuterie, cultivated during years coming up in kitchens in Boston and Portland. Originally the plan was to start a wholesale business of locally raised and cured meats, but through a few twists, he ended up starting a small retail deli in an offbeat part of Portland. Two years later he's expanded to a second location. Each deli includes cases stocked with hand-rolled pastas, house-made charcuterie, and sauces and relishes, which will soon be available bottled, as well as a market featuring high-quality and locally made grocery staples and a selection of beers and wine.

Living out his philosophy that local food doesn't need to be expensive or saved for special occasions, Sueltenfuss sources most of his ingredients from farmers in Maine and can often be found behind the counter breaking down whole sides of pork. Sandwiches, which range from braised rabbit to foraged mushroom, are built on locally baked bread and spiked with a smear of piquant spreads. The relishes featured here are deceptively simple to make, and though their ingredients are similar, their flavors are strikingly different. Their most popular use is on deli platters and sandwiches. For an Italian sandwich, toast a sub roll and top it with pepperoncini relish, vinegar pepper relish, sliced salami, mortadella and pepperoni, lettuce, tomato, pickles, onions, and provolone. For a vegetarian take, top with marinated mushrooms.

Note: Pepperoncini can be hot, so wear gloves when stemming them to avoid a burning feeling in your hands.

# VINEGAR PEPPER RELISH

(MAKES 2 CUPS)

2 pounds red bell pepper

1 small red onion

½ cup granulated sugar

2 tablespoons red wine vinegar

½–1 teaspoon salt, to taste

¼–½ teaspoon black pepper, to taste

Remove the stems and seeds from the bell peppers and cut into small dice. Peel the onion and dice to the same size.

In a heavy-bottomed saucepan, combine the sugar and vinegar, stirring until the mixture is the consistency of wet sand. Place the mixture over medium heat and cook until the sugar has liquefied, stirring constantly. Add the peppers and onion and cook, stirring frequently, until most of the liquid has thickened, 20 to 30 minutes. Season with salt and pepper.

Chill before serving. Store refrigerated in a glass jar or other airtight container for up to 2 weeks.

# PEPPERONCINI RELISH

(MAKES 1½ CUPS)

2 cups jarred pepperoncini

1 small red onion

½ cup granulated sugar

2 tablespoons apple cider vinegar

½–1 teaspoon salt, to taste

¼–½ teaspoon black pepper, to taste

Drain the pepperoncini and, wearing gloves, remove the stems. Place in the bowl of a food processor and pulse. Peel and finely dice the onion.

In a heavy-bottomed saucepan, combine the sugar and vinegar, stirring until the mixture is the consistency of wet sand. Place the mixture over medium heat and cook until the sugar has liquefied, stirring constantly. Add the peppers and onion and cook, stirring frequently, until most of the liquid has thickened, 20 to 30 minutes. Season with salt and pepper.

Chill before serving. Store refrigerated in a glass jar or other airtight container for up to 2 weeks.

# PICCOLO

**111 Middle Street**
(207) 747-5307
*piccolomaine.com*
Chef/Owners: Damian Sansonetti and Ilma Jeil Lopez

Under a turquoise awning celebrating *tavolo e famiglia*—table and family—this intimate twenty-seat restaurant serves up beautifully plated dishes inspired by the Central and Southern Italian home cooking that Chef Damian Sansonetti remembers from his childhood. Chef Sansonetti and his wife, Chef Ilma Jeil Lopez, are veterans of some of New York's most acclaimed restaurants—they met while working together in the kitchen at Daniel Boulud's DB Bistro—and Piccolo reflects their shared enthusiasm for traditional cooking with unexpected twists. In an atmosphere that is both refined and rustic, the menu changes daily but always includes an assortment of Italian cheese and cured meats, seasonal vegetables, and house-made pastas, sauces, and breads. A curated wine list focuses on difficult-to-find Italian varietals. Desserts from Chef Lopez, a two-time James Beard semifinalist for Outstanding Pastry Chef, round out each meal.

The Lamb Ragu featured here is one of Piccolo's signature dishes. Chef Sansonetti describes it as a tribute to both of his grandmothers: One kept a large kitchen garden and inspired his love of fresh vegetables, the other made meaty, long-simmering sauces and stews. Cavatelli are curled pasta shells, whose name translates to "little hollows," which hold sauce in their centers. A special pasta maker is required to shape them. If you don't have a cavatelli maker, you can substitute a high-quality store-bought cavatelli or other shell-shaped pasta, cooked according to package directions.

# CAVATELLI WITH LAMB RAGU, ORANGE, MINT, AND PECORINO

(MAKES 4–6 SERVINGS)

Cavatelli (see recipe below)

Lamb Ragu (see recipe below)

½ cup fresh shaved or finely grated Abruzzi pecorino, for serving

4–6 whole fresh mint leaves (see note)

Zest of 1 orange

½ cup red Cerignola olive slivers (or other large Italian olives such as Castelvetrano)

Note: Right before serving, finely slice fresh mint leaves into a chiffonade. If this is done too early, the leaves will brown.

## Cavatelli

5 cups (750 grams) "00" Italian flour (plus extra for rolling out)

9 whole eggs

3 tablespoons plus 1 teaspoon (50 grams) olive oil

**To make the pasta:** On a clean countertop, place the flour in a pile, making a well in the center for the eggs and oil.

In a medium bowl, whisk the eggs and oil together, then slowly begin incorporating the flour. Knead the dough until it has a nice sheen and is not too tacky to the touch. Cover the dough and let rest for 30 to 45 minutes.

Working in batches, roll the pasta dough into ¼-inch-long logs and lightly dust with flour. Roll through the cavatelli machine, adding more flour if needed to keep from sticking. Refrigerate shaped dough until ready to use.

## Lamb Ragu

3 tablespoons canola oil

1½ pounds ground lamb (preferably boneless neck meat or shoulder)

2 medium onions, chopped into medium dice

8 garlic cloves, minced

2 celery stalks, chopped into medium dice

3 carrots, scrubbed and chopped into medium dice

1 heaping tablespoon dried oregano (Sicilian is preferred)

2 teaspoons dried mint

1 teaspoon ground cayenne pepper

3 tablespoons tomato paste

1 cup dry red wine

2 cups lamb or beef stock

1½ quarts San Marzano pureed tomatoes

Kosher salt and freshly ground black pepper

**To make the sauce:** In a large, heavy-bottomed pot, heat the oil over high heat. Shape the ground lamb into thick patties, and sear on both sides until meat begins to brown. Remove patties from the pan, and set aside.

Add the onion, garlic, celery, and carrots to the pot and sweat them in the oil for 3 to 5 minutes. If the pan is dry, add more canola oil so that the vegetables don't stick. Stir in the dried spices.

Return the browned meat to the pan, and break into pieces with a wooden spoon. Stir in the tomato paste; cook, stirring constantly. Add the red wine and cook down the mixture, continuing to stir. Add the stock to the pot; cook for an additional 10 minutes, stirring constantly. Stir in the pureed tomatoes and season with salt and pepper to taste. Lower heat to medium-low and cook for about 1 hour, stirring occasionally to make sure that nothing sticks to the bottom.

**To prepare the dish:** Bring a large pot of salted water to a boil. Add the cavatelli and cook until tender, testing for doneness 2 to 3 minutes after the water has returned to boil.

Using a slotted spoon, remove pasta from the water and stir into the Lamb Ragu, cooking for an additional 5 to 10 minutes to let all the flavors come together.

Adjust seasoning before spooning into large bowls. Just before serving, garnish with a generous amount of grated pecorino, chiffonade of fresh mint leaves, a sprinkle of orange zest, and olive slivers.

# RICOTTA TART

(MAKES 1 8-INCH TART)

1 8-inch Tart Shell (see recipe below)

Ricotta Filling (see recipe below)

Vanilla Whipped Cream (see recipe below)

Maldon sea salt, for serving

Zest of one lemon, for serving

## Tart Shell

2 cups all-purpose flour

1 cup granulated sugar

1 teaspoon baking powder

½ cup unsalted butter, at room temperature

3 large eggs

1 tablespoon dark rum

**To make Tart Shell:** Combine all the ingredients in the bowl of a food processor. Pulse until just incorporated. Turn out the dough onto a lightly floured surface and knead until it comes together in a ball. Cover with plastic wrap and place in the refrigerator to rest and chill for at least 30 minutes.

When ready to use, roll out in a lightly floured surface and place dough into an 8-inch tart pan. Return to refrigerator to chill while preparing the filling.

## Ricotta Filling

1 pound ricotta

1 cup granulated sugar

2 large eggs

6 egg yolks

2 tablespoons rum

½ tablespoon pure vanilla extract

Confectioners' sugar

**To make Ricotta Filling:** Combine the ricotta, sugar, eggs, egg yolks, rum, and vanilla extract in the bowl of a food processor and pulse until well incorporated. Pour the mixture into the chilled Tart Shell and return to the refrigerator.

**To make the tart:** Preheat oven to 350°F. Bake tart for 30 minutes, until the middle is set and top is golden. Cool to room temperature before serving.

To serve, lightly dust the top of the tart with confectioners' sugar. Place a small dot of Vanilla Whipped Cream on each plate before setting down a slice of tart (this will secure the slice so it doesn't slide around). Top each serving with a dollop of Vanilla Whipped Cream, and sprinkle with lemon zest and a few flakes of sea salt.

## Vanilla Whipped Cream

1 cup heavy cream

1 teaspoon sugar

1 teaspoon pure vanilla extract

**To make Vanilla Whipped Cream:** In a small bowl, combine cream, sugar, and vanilla extract. Use a whisk or electric mixer to whip until the cream holds a soft point. Use immediately.

# PIZZARINO

505 Fore Street
(207) 536-1189
*pizzarino.us*
Chef/Owner: Mauro Stoppani
Co-Owner: Enrico Barbiero

This casual pizza restaurant at the edge of the Old Port is the creation of two high school friends from Milan, who've teamed up to offer the flavors of home: authentic Italian wood-fired pizzas, risotto, gnocchi, and salads. The pizzeria's expansive space, in a brick building down the street from co-owner Enrico Barbiero's first restaurant, Paciarino, is comfortable and inviting. Patrons are likely to be greeted at the door by pizza master Mauro Stoppani, whose enthusiasm is underscored by his extensive study of pizza-making techniques. Chef Stoppani's attention begins with the flour used to make the crust—at Pizzarino they use a blend endorsed by the Italian University of Gastronomic Sciences, which they import from Italy and have available for sale by the bag. The process of making the crust is meticulous, and temperatures and leavening times are precisely calculated and monitored. This results in pizzas that are fragrant and light, topped with imported Italian tomatoes, cheeses, and meats, best paired with one of the imported Italian wines, beers, or sodas on offer.

## PROSCIUTTO COTTO PIZZA

### (MAKES 5 INDIVIDUAL-SERVING PIZZAS)

To make Pizzarino's Proscuitto Cotto Pizza, it is best to use an imported whole meal flour blend, available at Italian groceries and online. For pizza that is *Italiani autentici*, use imported meats and cheeses, but high-quality domestic products are a fine substitute.

Dough

2⅓ cups (550 grams) water

6⅓ cups (1 kilogram) whole Special Italian Flour

¼ teaspoon (1 gram) fresh yeast

1½ tablespoons (27 grams) salt

2 tablespoons (27 grams) extra virgin olive oil

In a large bowl, combine the water, 3 cups of flour, and the yeast, and mix by hand to incorporate. Cover, and allow the dough to rest at room temperature (approximately 68°F) overnight, to double in size.

When dough has doubled in size, turn out onto a lightly floured surface, and knead in the remaining flour. When the dough is smooth and the flour is fully incorporated, add the salt and knead to distribute. After 5 minutes of kneading, drizzle the oil over the dough, and continue to knead (the dough will get a little slippery, but continue kneading until the oil is fully incorporated).

Cover the dough and let it rest at room temperature for an hour. Divide the dough into 5 equal parts, and shape each into a ball. Place dough balls in a large bowl, cover, and refrigerate for 12 hours until ready to use.

### Pizza

Rice flour

½ cup (120 grams) Italian tomato sauce (season tomato sauce with salt, pepper, basil, garlic, and spices, if you'd like)

1½ cups (160 grams) fresh Italian mozzarella cheese, diced

¾ cup (120 grams) fresh Italian prosciutto cotto ham, sliced

When you're ready to make the pizzas, remove the dough from the refrigerator and allow to come to room temperature (this will take about 1 hour). Preheat oven to 480 degrees.

Dust your work surface with rice flour and, working with one ball at a time, begin stretching the dough, creating a wheel with a diameter of about 13 inches. Try not to touch the perimeter, or the parts of the crust that will be uncovered.

Spoon approximately 1½ tablespoons of tomato sauce into the center of the dough, and use a spatula to spread it in a thin layer. Top with ⅕ of the cheese and ham.

Bake pizzas at 480 degrees for about 10 minutes, until crust is baked and cheese is bubbly. Alternatively, if you have a wood-fired brick oven, heat it to 850 degrees and bake pizzas for 3 minutes each.

# THE PORTLAND HUNT AND ALPINE CLUB

75 Market Street
(207) 747-4754
*huntandalpineclub.com*
Co-Owners: Andrew and Briana Volk
Bartenders: Tyler Schweppes and Trey Hughes

With the air of a modern ski lodge—white walls, stained woods, mounted wire animal heads, and a few darkly atmospheric still lifes—the Portland Hunt and Alpine Club opened to much excitement in 2013. Serving beautifully crafted cocktails and a Scandinavian-inspired menu of heavy snacks and light meals, this Old Port establishment is the embodiment of co-owners Andrew and Briana Volk's ethos of northern hospitality, a custom the couple has popularized in their book of the same name. It's also earned them accolades, from magazines like *Bon Appetit* and *Food and Wine*, and two times as James Beard semifinalists for Outstanding Bar Program, in 2015 and 2017.

Patrons crowd the long communal tables and metal-topped bar, or huddle in a wood-paneled private side room reminiscent of a sauna, choosing cocktails with such witty and vivid descriptions that you want to order them all. From the kitchen, dishes with Scandinavian roots appear alongside classic bar snacks: Gravlax, smorgasbord, and Swedish meatballs share the table with house-made pretzels, spiced popcorn, and a daily deviled egg. Above all, this is a connoisseur's bar, and knowledgeable, enthusiastic staff are happy to answer questions about the multipage list of spirits, which includes three absinthes and a half page designated "rare + obscure."

## CLOVE HITCH

### (MAKES 1 SERVING)

1½ ounces tequila

¾ ounce St. George Spiced Pear

½ ounce lime juice

½ ounce grapefruit juice

½ ounce agave nectar

Lime wheel, for garnish

Combine all liquid ingredients with cracked ice in a cocktail shaker. Shake well. Strain into a martini glass and garnish with a lime wheel.

## LATE NIGHT AT OPT

### (MAKES 1 SERVING)

¾ ounce Absolut citron

½ ounce lime juice

¼ ounce Pierre Ferrand Dry Curacao

¼ ounce cranberry juice

Pint glass two-thirds full with pilsner beer

Combine first four ingredients with cracked ice in a cocktail shaker. Shake well and strain into a shot glass. Before serving, drop shot glass into the beer.

# RIFLE TALK

(MAKES 1 SERVING)

2 ounces Plantation dark rum

¾ ounce Allen's Coffee-Flavored Brandy

¼ ounce Becherovka

1 dash Angostura bitters

Combine all ingredients with cracked ice in a cocktail shaker. Shake well. Strain into a martini glass.

# ROSE FOODS

428 Forest Avenue
(207) 835-0991
*rosefoods.me*
Chef/Owner: Chad Conley
Chef: Matt Jatczak
Baker: Kevin Gravito

A short jog off the peninsula, from a brick storefront on a bustling stretch of Forest Avenue, the smell of golden bagels wafts through the air. Rose Foods, conceived by restaurateur Chef Chad Conley, is a classic Jewish deli and bagel shop that opened in the summer of 2017 to much anticipation and acclaim—in their first few weeks, lines stretched past the tiled threshold and far down the block before the bakery doors opened. Chef Conley's career has ranged from fine dining at Portland's Hugo's and New York's Jean George to farming at Eliot Coleman's famed Four Season Farm in Harborside, Maine. But his heart has stayed true to impeccably done classic American cuisine. Conley's first restaurant, Biddeford's celebrated Palace Diner, gained national attention with its stacks of fluffy pancakes, mile-high sandwiches, and luscious banana bread, earning a James Beard nomination in 2019.

Rose Foods similarly hearkens back to a previous era, with appetizing deli specialties like latkes, house-cured pastrami and lox, generous shmears of schmaltz (rendered chicken fat), and gribenes (crispy bits of oniony chicken skin), offset by whole grain health bread and, of course, bagels baked fresh every morning. The atmosphere is open and warm, with shelves filled with cans of Dr. Brown's Cel-Ray and cream soda, self-service water and cutlery, and a back room reminiscent of an old-time cafeteria, with cozily low ceilings, black-and-white photos, and accent walls covered in bright vintage wallpaper prints. If you're lucky enough to get a table during the busy morning rush, a stranger might join you at one of the cheerful Formica tables.

Using a sourdough starter and rye soaker, the Deli Rye Bread Loaf (featured here) is a two-day process (more if you need to make the starter), and requires patience and some advanced knowledge of yeast doughs. Dough conditioner, called for in this recipe, builds a beautiful texture in the bread and can be ordered online. At Rose Foods, Deli Rye is the base of many favorite sandwiches—top with pastrami or corned beef, or serve alongside a hearty soup.

# ROSE LOX

## (MAKES 1 SIDE OF SALMON)

1 side salmon (roughly 3–3½ pounds)

2¼ cups kosher salt

1½ cups light brown sugar

1½ cups granulated sugar

Zest of 2 lemons

Zest of 1 grapefruit

Zest of 3 oranges

7 teaspoons fennel seeds, ground

4 teaspoons caraway seeds, ground

4 tablespoons coriander seeds, ground

1 bunch fresh dill, chopped

Rinse side of salmon and pat dry with a paper towel. Set aside on a baking sheet, and refrigerate until ready to use.

In a medium-size bowl, combine kosher salt, sugars, citrus zest, and ground spices. Mix well, making sure there are no clumps of brown sugar or zest.

Sprinkle chopped dill over the flesh of the salmon and wrap the fish in cheesecloth. On a rimmed baking sheet, sprinkle a thin layer of the salt mixture, and then lay the cheesecloth-wrapped salmon skin-side down on the salt mixture. Cover the fish with the rest of the mixture, making sure it is entirely covered and there is no piece of fish exposed (this will ensure even, proper curing). Place a piece of parchment paper over the top of the fish and put at least 10 pounds of weight on top of the fish. Let the fish rest in the refrigerator under the weight for 4 days.

Remove the fish from the cure, unwrap it from the cheesecloth, and slice thinly. Rose Lox will keep in the refrigerator for up to 3 weeks.

# POTATO KNISHES

(MAKES 8 SERVINGS)

## Dough

3 cups bread flour

1 teaspoon baking powder

1 teaspoon salt

1 egg

½ cup schmaltz

Scant ½ teaspoon malt vinegar

½ cup water

**To make the dough:** Place all ingredients in the bowl of a stand mixer. With the paddle attachment, beat until thoroughly combined, 3 to 4 minutes. Scrape down the sides and shape the dough into a ball. Wrap in plastic wrap and set aside. Place in the refrigerator and allow dough to rest for at least 1 hour before rolling out.

## Potato Filling

4½ teaspoons unsalted butter

4½ teaspoons canola oil

2 large Yukon Gold potatoes, peeled and diced

1 large white onion, diced

1½ bunches scallions, trimmed and sliced

2 cups water

1½ teaspoons dried sage

½ teaspoon freshly ground black pepper

1 tablespoon salt

1 tablespoon malt vinegar

1½ cups shredded cheddar cheese, plus more for sprinkling

1 egg beaten with 1 tablespoon cool water, for egg wash

**To make Potato Filling:** In a large pot over low heat, warm butter and oil until butter is melted. Add potatoes, onions, and scallions, and cook until vegetables are soft, about 20 minutes. Add water, sage, pepper, salt, and malt vinegar. Raise heat to medium, and cook for another 30 minutes, until half the liquid has evaporated. Using an immersion blender, puree potato mixture until smooth. (Alternatively, place the potato mixture in a blender or the bowl of a food processor and blend until smooth.) Mix in the shredded cheese. Taste for seasoning, adjusting salt and pepper to taste.

**To assemble the knishes:** Preheat oven to 350°F. Line a baking sheet with parchment paper. Remove dough from refrigerator and, with a knife or bench scraper, divide chilled dough into thirds. Place one-third of the dough on a floured surface, returning the rest to the refrigerator. Roll out the dough until you have a rectangle roughly 12 x 16 inches. The dough should be relatively thin.

With the long side of the dough facing you, spoon 2-tablespoon portions of potato filling along the bottom edge of the dough, leaving a few inches between each scoop. Fold the dough over the filling and roll up until there are three layers of dough. Trim any excess dough.

Pinch dough in between portions of filling and cut apart the portions. Twist and pinch each end shut to enclose the filling. Place each knish on the prepared baking sheet, with the pinched part up, and gently press down until the knish is completely sealed. Continue with remaining dough.

When you're ready to bake, brush each knish with egg wash, and sprinkle with grated cheddar cheese. Bake for 40 minutes, until dough is golden.

# DELI RYE BREAD LOAF

(MAKES 4 LOAVES)

Sourdough starters can be made at home by combining whole wheat or rye flour and water and allowing it to ferment. Once it begins to bubble, it must be tended by feeding it with unbleached flour. Live starter can also be ordered online.

Rye Soaker (see recipe below)

Sourdough Mixture (see recipe below)

11 cups bread flour

1¾ teaspoons active dry yeast

3 tablespoons caraway seeds

5 teaspoons salt

2 tablespoons dough conditioner

1¼ teaspoons malt extract

### Rye Soaker

Scant 3 cups cubed day-old rye bread

⅓ cup, plus 1 tablespoon hot water

The day before baking, make the rye soaker. In a large, nonreactive pot with a lid, cover the day-old rye bread cubes with the hot water. Cover, and allow to sit overnight.

### Sourdough Mixture

5½ cups water

7 cups, plus 1 tablespoon rye flour

2½ teaspoons sourdough starter

In a large bowl, combine water, rye flour, and sourdough starter. Mix to incorporate, cover loosely with plastic wrap, and allow to sit overnight.

To make the bread: On the day of baking, place rye soaker, sourdough mixture, and remaining ingredients in the bowl of a stand mixer fitted with a dough hook; beat on low for 10 minutes.

Grease a large bowl. Once dough is thoroughly incorporated, place in the greased bowl, folding the dough over once on itself. Cover loosely and allow to rise, in a warm place, for 30 minutes. While dough is rising, line two baking sheets with parchment paper and spray with cooking oil.

When dough has risen, divide into four pieces. Allow dough to rest 10 minutes, then shape each loaf into a loose round. Let dough rest, covered, another 30 minutes.

Roll each piece of dough into a long loaf (a *batard*), arranging them on the pans so that they have plenty of room to expand. Allow loaves to rise, covered, for an additional 30 minutes.

While dough is rising, preheat oven to 450°F. Make sure that racks are arranged so that loaves have ample room to expand. Place sheets in the oven and immediately lower temperature to 325°F. Bake for 30 minutes. Rotate the baking sheets and lower the temperature to 300°F. Bake for an additional 15 minutes. Bread is done when loaves sound hollow when rapped on the bottom.

Remove bread from baking sheets and place on a wire rack to cool. Allow to cool completely before slicing. Extra loaves can be wrapped tightly in plastic wrap and frozen until ready to use.

# HOUSE-CURED CHARCUTERIE

Maine's tradition of curing meats and fish goes back centuries, to the Native American techniques chronicled by Henry David Thoreau in his travel classic, *The Maine Woods*: "Two stout forked stakes . . . were driven into the ground at each end, and then two poles ten feet long were stretched across over the fire, and smaller ones laid transversely on these a foot apart. On the last hung large, thin slices of moose-meat smoking and drying . . . over the centre of the fire." Though modern meat preservation is more likely to involve Insta-cure ordered online and a metal smoker, the enthusiasm for house-cured meats has been revived throughout Portland's restaurant kitchens. From pork and beef to freshwater trout, cured meats and fish are emerging from smokers, drying rooms, and walk-in refrigerators throughout the city.

# Salvage Barbecue

919 Congress Street
(207) 553-2100
*salvagebbq.com*
Chef/Owner: Jay Villani
Co-Owner: Garry Bowcott

In an open, expansive space, carved from a renovated railroad post office building a few blocks from the Portland Seadog's Hadlock Field, this quick service restaurant was among the first to popularize Southern-style barbecue in Maine. Before opening, chef/owner Jay Villani and his team took an eating tour of the Carolinas and Texas, searching for inspiration, and they returned to Portland ready to share what they'd learned. Opened in 2012, the space is filled with long communal tables, each topped with a caddy of sauces and rolls of paper towels. Order at the counter—meats can be ordered separately or in combinations like the "Meat Coma" and "Meat Fatality," and sides are bought by the pint or quart—and play a vintage arcade game or listen to live bluegrass or honky-tonk music while you wait. The smoke shack out back perfumes the neighborhood, and regulars come in for bingo (Sunday), for trivia nights (Wednesday), or to simply watch the game with a pint at the restaurant's large bar.

The main event at Salvage is the meat—rubbed with spices and barbecued, low and slow, in their custom-built smokers. The Evil Death Slather (E-D-S) sauces are made in house, and Salvage now has a selection of eleven, with rotating seasonal offerings. Evil Death Slather #6 (also known as Blueberry Hot Sauce) is hot and spicy, with a fruitiness that still shines through. It's crafted for smoked meats but pairs nicely with any grilled foods.

Corn bread muffins, a staple on any barbecue menu, are best right out of the oven, but leftovers can be buttered and toasted on a griddle, or crumbled and frozen for stuffing. The secret to Salvage's tender crumb is to let the batter sit in the refrigerator overnight, making this a great muffin to serve at brunch. For a fun twist, add a generous handful of chopped pickled jalapeños, smoked pecans, or minced dried fruit to the batter.

# EVIL DEATH SLATHER #6 (BLUEBERRY HOT SAUCE)

## (MAKES 2 16-OUNCE JARS)

1½ cups blueberries

1 cup fresh lemon juice

1 cup fresh habanero peppers, de-stemmed

¼ cup red wine vinegar

2 cups sugar

Pinch of salt

Combine all ingredients in the bowl of a food processor or blender, blend on high until pureed. Pour into sterilized 16-ounce mason jars, or other tight-lidded, nonreactive containers, and let marinate overnight. Sauce will keep in the refrigerator for up to 1 week.

# CORNBREAD MUFFINS

## (MAKES 2 DOZEN MUFFINS)

½ cup, plus 1½ tablespoons unsalted butter

2 large eggs, at room temperature

½ cup granulated or turbinado sugar

1 cup buttermilk, at room temperature for
   30 minutes

2 cups all-purpose flour

2 cups cornmeal

⅓ teaspoon salt

⅓ teaspoon baking soda

In a small saucepan over low heat, melt butter until it runs freely but isn't too hot to touch. In the bowl of a stand mixer fitted with a paddle attachment, combine melted butter, eggs, and sugar, and beat at medium speed until mixture is uniform, 3 to 5 minutes. Slowly add buttermilk and mix for an additional 2 to 3 minutes, until well incorporated.

In a separate medium-size bowl, combine dry ingredients and whisk to mix. With the mixer on low, slowly add the dry mixture to the wet, and beat until thoroughly incorporated. Cover bowl tightly with plastic wrap (or pour batter into a separate container with a tight lid) and store in the refrigerator overnight.

When you are ready to bake, preheat oven to 400°F. Grease two muffin pans liberally with butter or shortening. Scoop ⅓ cup of cold batter into each muffin tin. Immediately place pans on the center rack of the preheated oven. Note: It is important to portion the batter while it's cold and put the muffin pans straight into the oven to prevent your batter from breaking. If batter breaks, the butter will run out, leading to a flat, dense muffin.

Bake muffins for 20 minutes. Muffins are ready when a toothpick or cake tester inserted into the center of a muffin comes out clean. Cool muffins on a wire rack for 20 to 30 minutes before serving.

# FORAGING FIDDLEHEADS, MUSHROOMS, RAMPS

For those who know where to look, Maine's forests, fields, and stream banks can provide a bountiful feast. Some of Maine's earthiest and most iconic flavors—from spring's first fiddlehead ferns and wild ramps to autumn's delicate black trumpet mushrooms—are foraged from spots carefully guarded through generations. A fixture on the Portland culinary scene, forager Rick Tibbetts scours southern Maine for these incredible edibles, bringing his haul of unusual fungi and ferns to the area's best restaurants. Delicious on the menu, these natural wonders can also be found at better markets around town. Tempting though it may be to try foraging on your own, it's a skill that requires years of training, and a single false identification can be toxic. Aspiring foragers do best to go on a guided walk with an expert or to join a foraging club like the Maine Mycological Association (mushroomthejournal.com).

# SCALES

**Maine Wharf**
**68 Commercial Street**
**(207) 805-0444**
*scalesrestaurant.com*
Owner: Dana Street
Chefs: Frederic Eliot and Travis Olson

Past a row of pilings and through the weathered door on a wharf jutting into the working water-front, the cavernous dining room at Scales is best described as a New England brasserie. With a menu of French-leaning variations on Maine classics, a generous raw bar of oysters, littleneck clams, and an assortment of tartares and ceviches, and the occasional *pâté en croûte*, Scales is a celebration of the sea and coast. A wall of windows overlooks the water, and on busy summer evenings, patrons fill the driftwood-topped booths, stand two deep at the long bar, and watch as chefs pull live lobsters from the poured concrete tanks at the front of the kitchen. Periodically, cascades of ice cubes are released from a chute in the ceiling to refresh the raw bar's bed of ice.

Cast iron pans hang in a row, framing the visible kitchen, run jointly by Chefs Fred Eliot and Travis Olson. Chef Eliot, who hails from France by way of New York City and the kitchen at Le Cirque, puts an unmistakable French stamp on his preparations of the daily catch. His Baked Haddock recipe is inspired by a dish from the famed restaurant, Troisgros, in Lyons, France. The rich fumet cream sauce is brightened by a final touch of lemon. While the recipe calls for meaty chanterelles, seasonal mushrooms such as spring morels and summer black trumpets can be substituted.

Chef Olson, a trained pastry chef who spent time in the kitchen at Copenhagen's Noma and at Washington, D.C.'s hyper-local Glen's Garden Market, brings a love of vegetables, working with local growers to find the perfect varieties for each dish. His preferred kohlrabi for the salad featured here is Kossak, which stays crisp and tender as it grows to an enormous eight pounds. A great keeper, Kossak kohlrabi can be carved and used a quarter at a time. Flavorful and aromatic American black walnuts are available at specialty shops and can be ordered online. Chef Olson's preferred nuts come from Hammons, a Midwestern company specializing in sustainably raised and hand-harvested black walnuts.

# KOHLRABI SALAD

(MAKES 4 SERVINGS)

¼ of a large (6–8 pounds whole) kohlrabi

Salt, to taste

4 stalks celery, plus some leaves

½ of a bunch flat-leaf parsley

¼ cup American black walnut pieces

2 ounces aged (2–3 years) Gouda cheese

Lemon Vinaigrette (see recipe below)

Freshly ground black pepper, to taste

Trim the stem and root ends off the kohlrabi with a heavy knife. Stand it on end for stability while trimming the remaining skin away. Cut the trimmed kohlrabi in half, then lay it down on its cut face and cut in half again. Now take one of the quarter pieces and slice it into ¼-inch-wide planks. Shave the planks carefully on a mandoline slicer to resemble fettucine noodles.

In a large bowl, season the kohlrabi to taste with salt and set aside. The salt will make the strips pliable and tender after a few minutes, but this step can be done several hours in advance of serving.

Slice the celery stalks thinly on a bias to create chevron shapes. Pick leaves of celery and parsley, discarding stems.

Preheat oven to 300°F. Place black walnuts on a rimmed baking sheet and toast for 6 to 8 minutes, until fragrant. Check after 5 minutes to ensure that they do not brown. When cool, chop them up a bit smaller so they will cling to the salad.

Shave the Gouda with a vegetable peeler, or use a sharp knife.

To prepare the salad, toss the ingredients together with the Lemon Vinaigrette in a large bowl. Adjust to taste with salt and plenty of freshly ground black pepper.

## Lemon Vinaigrette

½ clove garlic, shaved on a microplane or crushed to a paste with the side of a knife

Juice of 1 lemon

1 tablespoon pure maple syrup

½ teaspoon salt

¼ cup extra virgin olive oil

In a small bowl, whisk ingredients vigorously until thoroughly combined.

## BAKED HADDOCK WITH FUMET SAUCE

### (MAKES 4 SERVINGS)

4 leeks

4 tablespoons unsalted butter, divided

Salt and freshly ground black pepper, to taste

12 fingerling potatoes

Sprig of fresh thyme

1 clove garlic, crushed, with skin on

½ pound seasonal wild mushrooms (morels, black trumpets, or chanterelles)

Fumet Cream Sauce (see recipe below)

4 (6-ounce) fillets of haddock, cleaned and patted dry

Chopped fresh parsley

**To prepare the vegetables:** Thoroughly clean the leeks under cold water, removing the outer layer and rinsing any grit trapped between the layers. Slice leeks into 1-inch cylinders.

In a sauté pan, melt 2 tablespoons of butter. Add sliced leeks and a splash of water. Season with salt and pepper and cook gently over low heat until leeks are meltingly soft and not fibrous. Set aside.

In a medium pot, cover fingerling potatoes with cold water and season heavily with salt. The water should taste like sea water. Add thyme and crushed garlic. Bring water to a boil and let simmer until potatoes are cooked through. When poked with a sharp paring knife, the potatoes should slide right off and not stick. Drain and set aside.

Clean the mushrooms thoroughly. If using chanterelles, peel and trim the stems. If using morels, slice in half lengthwise. Black trumpets can be left whole. Wash the mushrooms quickly in a cold-water bath that is deep enough that the mushrooms can float and let any dirt settle at the bottom. Remove from water and dry gently on a kitchen towel. In a sauté pan, melt remaining 2 tablespoons of butter and cook mushrooms briefly, seasoning with salt to draw out moisture. Set aside.

## Fumet Cream Sauce

½ cup brunoise shallot (⅛-inch dice)

6 tablespoons unsalted butter

1 cup white wine

2 cups Fumet (see recipe below)

2 tablespoons all-purpose flour

1 cup milk

3 cups heavy cream

Salt, to taste

Freshly squeezed lemon juice

**To make Fumet Cream Sauce:** In a braiser or rondeau pan over low heat, sweat the shallots in butter until translucent. Add white wine, raise heat to medium-high, and cook until liquid is almost entirely cooked off.

Add Fumet, and cook down again until completely reduced. Stir in the flour, reduce heat to low, and cook for 2 to 3 minutes.

Whisk in the milk and cook, stirring continually, until the mixture starts to thicken from the flour. Stir in the heavy cream, 1 cup at a time, making sure that the mixture comes to a simmer before adding the next cup. (Adding the cream gradually will prevent any burning of the flour mixture at the bottom of the pan.) Season with salt to taste and a dash of lemon juice. Refrigerate, if not using immediately.

## Fumet

1 cup diced white mirepoix (see note)

1 tablespoon vegetable oil

Body of 1 fresh white fish, bones and head, rinsed

1 bunch fresh thyme

3 fresh bay leaves

1 tablespoon black peppercorns

1 clove garlic, crushed

1 cup dry white wine

Cold water

Note: White mirepoix is a mixture of celery, onions, and fennel bulb, diced into ¼-inch cubes.

**To make Fumet:** In a stock pot or other large, heavy-bottomed pot, sauté mirepoix in vegetable oil until vegetables are translucent. Add fish body, bones, and head, thyme, bay leaves, peppercorns, and crushed garlic; cook on medium heat for 5 to 10 minutes. Deglaze the pan with white wine, using a wooden spoon to scrape up any bits that may have stuck to the bottom. Add enough cold water to cover the fish bones, and bring to a simmer. Leave at a low simmer for about 45 minutes, skimming off any foam that rises to the surface. Strain through a fine sieve, and refrigerate if not using immediately.

**To assemble the dish:** Preheat oven to 450°F. Season each fillet of fish with salt and pepper. In a baking dish, for each fillet, pour ½ cup of Fumet Cream Sauce (freshly made or pulled from the refrigerator an hour before use). Place the seasoned haddock fillet on top and cover each piece of fish with an additional generous ¼ cup ladle of sauce. Nestle leeks, potatoes, and mushrooms among the fillets.

Place baking dish in the oven for about 10 minutes (or longer, depending on the thickness of the fillet), or until the cream bubbles vigorously. Test the fish for doneness by inserting the tip of a sharp knife into the thickest part of the fillet. Before serving, garnish with chopped parsley.

# SOLO ITALIANO

100 Commercial Street
(207) 780-0227
*soloitalianorestaurant.com*
Chef/Owner: Paolo Laboa
Co-Owner: Mercedes Laboa

Incorporating seasonal Maine ingredients into classic Italian cooking is the defining principle of Chef Paolo Laboa's *cucina* at Solo Italiano. Set on a corner of Commercial Street, patrons can choose between two dining rooms: an open room with tall windows and mural-lined walls near the kitchen and crudo station, or a more intimate area by the bar, with a few lucky tables overlooking the working waterfront. The restaurant is a family affair—Chef Laboa and his wife and co-owner, Mercedes, met when she was his sous chef at Farina in San Francisco, and the menu, which changes daily, reflects a familial ease. Long-simmering sauces, fresh pastas flecked with herbs, and hearty seafood stews reflect Chef Laboa's Genovese roots.

Named the Best Young Chef in Italy in 1992, Chef Laboa earned a Michelin star while executive chef at Gran Gotto in Genoa. In 2008 he was named the World Pesto Champion. For all his accolades, Chef Laboa approaches the kitchen with humility and unbridled enthusiasm for the local flavors, describing himself as simply a "creative vessel for the ingredients coming from the land and sea." He is also a willing teacher, and the restaurant holds monthly pasta-making classes, where students can learn at his side. House-made pastas, seasonal panettone, and Chef Laboa's famed pesto are also available to take home from a retail space at the restaurant.

Solo Italiano's Lobster and Borage Lasagna takes advantage of the fresh herbs and seafood found in Maine. With edible sky-blue flowers and a slight hint of cucumber, borage is a favorite

culinary and medicinal herb, found locally at its peak in August. If borage is not available, chard or spinach leaves can be substituted. This pasta is versatile and can be made into other shapes and served with a simple butter or cream sauce.

*Tocco* is a traditional, long-simmered meat sauce from Genoa, similar to a ragu. This sauce, made with lobster bodies, is velvety smooth and strained before use. Like the pasta, the sauce is versatile and can be used in other dishes.

A note on homemade pasta: The texture and consistency of pasta dough can be affected by slight variations in the ingredients and humidity. Make sure to use 00 durum flour, available in specialty shops and online, and experiment with the dough until it is firm and moist, somewhat elastic, and doesn't stick to your fingers when you work it.

# LOBSTER AND BORAGE LASAGNA

(MAKES 6-8 SERVINGS)

Borage Pasta Dough (see recipe below)

Lobster Tocco Sauce (see recipe below)

Béchamel (see recipe below)

Reserved lobster meat

½ cup grated Parmigiano-Reggiano cheese, or more to taste

Fresh borage blossoms, for garnish

## Borage Pasta Dough

1½ cups (300 grams) blanched borage leaves, squeezed to reduce excess water

7 cups (800 grams) 00 durum flour

Small ½ bunch of marjoram, leaves stripped from stems

5 large eggs

**To make Borage Pasta Dough:** In the bowl of a food processor, grind borage leaves until finely chopped. Place all ingredients in a large bowl and knead by hand until thoroughly incorporated. If dough seems too crumbly and doesn't stick together, add another whole egg. Dough will be ready when it is firm, springy, and moist, but doesn't stick to your fingers. Cover with a damp towel and allow dough to rest for 10 minutes.

Working in batches, run dough through a pasta machine, making long sheets on the thinnest setting. Pasta strips should be approximately 5 inches wide and 12 to 13 inches long. Using a sharp knife or pizza cutter, trim pasta to size. When finished, you should have fourteen strips. Set finished pasta on a rack or a piece of flour-dusted parchment paper until ready to proceed.

## Lobster Tocco Sauce

2 lobster bodies and heads, claw and tail meat removed, steamed and set aside

Extra virgin olive oil

2–3 garlic cloves

Sprig of fresh rosemary

3 fresh sage leaves

10–12 San Marzano or Roma tomatoes, chopped

Salt and freshly ground black pepper, to taste

**To make Lobster Tocco Sauce:** In a large, heavy-bottomed pot over medium heat, cook lobster shells and heads with a generous pour of olive oil. When fragrant, add herbs and chopped tomatoes. Reduce heat, bringing mixture to a simmer, and cook for 1½ to 2 hours, until sauce tastes rich and flavorful. Adjust seasonings to taste. Remove from heat and strain sauce through a fine sieve. Set aside.

## Béchamel

2¼ cups whole milk, farm fresh if possible

⅓ cup unsalted butter, from pastured cows,
    if possible

⅓ cup 00 durum flour

Salt, to taste

Freshly grated nutmeg, to taste

**To make the béchamel:** In a small saucepan over medium-high heat, bring milk to a boil. In a separate saucepan, over medium heat, melt butter. When butter is completely melted and foam begins to subside, pour in all the flour. Add salt and nutmeg; whisk vigorously, cooking for a few minutes but making sure the mixture doesn't brown. Pour hot milk over the butter–flour mixture, whisking to integrate all the ingredients. Bring to a slight boil, stirring continuously. Béchamel is ready when it has thickened.

**To make the lasagna:** Bring a large pot of salted water to a boil. Working in batches, cook the lasagna noodles until they are al dente, making sure not to overcook. Lay cooked noodles flat on a baking sheet until you are ready to assemble the lasagna.

Preheat oven to 350°F. In a 9- x 13-inch ceramic or glass baking dish, spread a layer of Lobster Tocco Sauce, a layer of béchamel, and cover with two strips of pasta. Follow with béchamel sauce, tocco, and a touch of grated Parmigiano-Reggiano, to taste. Repeat five times, finishing with a layer of béchamel and tocco. Top with steamed lobster meat.

Cook for 10 minutes, then let sit for 2 hours (or overnight) to allow flavors to meld and mature. Before serving, bake, uncovered, at 350°F, until lasagna is piping hot and top is crisped. Serve garnished with fresh borage blossoms and grated or shaved Parmigiano-Reggiano.

# THE PORTLAND FARMERS' MARKET

Founded in 1768, the Portland Farmers' Market has the distinction of being one of the oldest continually operating farmers' markets in the country. Originally housed in the lower floor of the Town Hall, the market began as a central location for the peddlers who went door-to-door selling lobsters, mollusks, and fresh vegetables from makeshift carts. First created to serve the 136 families who lived on the peninsula, it was in its early years by ordinance Portland's exclusive source of fresh meat. In 1805 the market moved to Monument Square (then called Hay Market Square), and though the next century and a half brought several more moves, the Farmers' Market returned to Monument Square in 1990, where it has stayed ever since, expanding on summer Saturdays to include a morning market in Deering Oaks Park. The weekly market continues through the winter, when it moves off the peninsula to a location on Stevens Avenue. Today it's going strong, serving the entire Portland area, with nearly fifty farmers and artisans selling everything from pasture-raised pork to lacto-fermented vegetables and homemade face creams to handcrafted birdhouses.

# SUR LIE

**11 Free Street**
**(207) 956-7350**
*sur-lie.com*
Owners: Krista Cole and Antonio Alvarez
Chef: Emil Rivera

Opened in 2014, Sur Lie takes its name from a vintner's technique for aging wines—a hint at the restaurant's deep list of wines by the glass and bottle. More than a wine bar, however, the intimate, two-chambered space tucked on a quiet side street serves tapas-style dining with a narrative arc: The menu is organized like a timeline, beginning with a section "To Settle and Nibble," and ending with "Closure," a selection of desserts. In between, small plates are designated "Crisp," "Pleasant," and "Bold," and feature such dishes as salt-roasted beets with turmeric buttermilk dressing, parsnips and eggs with carrot caramel, blue spruce ash and pea tendrils, and Brussels sprouts with lardons and Marcona almonds, a favorite that's been on the menu since the restaurant opened.

Before coming to Portland and becoming, in his words, a "Puerto-Mainer," Chef Emil Rivera spent four years working with acclaimed Chef Jose Andres at his award-winning Washington D.C. tapas restaurant, Jaleo. Having honed his skills in that fast-paced kitchen, Chef Rivera now combines classic techniques with diverse flavors, offering beautifully prepared dishes for an eclectic palate. His approach has earned the restaurant accolades—Sur Lie was named Down East's Best New Restaurant of 2015—and led to an invitation for Chef Rivera to cook at the James Beard house in 2018.

A traditional Catalan dish similar to paella, rossejat is traditionally made with seafood, but can also include sausage. Chef Rivera makes it two ways, one with shrimp and the other with kielbasa; both versions are featured here. The noodles are first toasted to develop a round, nutty flavor, and are then cooked in stock until tender. The dish is meant to be cooked in a large paella pan or skillet, but can be made in individual pans. Sofrito, a classic in Spanish and Latin American cooking, is a versatile sauce and can be used to enrich rice, broths, seafood, and meats.

Pimentón de la Vera can be found in the spice section of most grocery stores. Piquillo peppers and trout roe, both used in the Russian Potato Salad, are available at gourmet grocers and online.

# ROSSEJAT

(MAKES 6–8 SERVINGS)

1 pound angel hair pasta

12–16 jumbo head-on shrimp or 1½ pounds kielbasa

1 cup Onion Sofrito (see recipe below)

4 cups Shrimp Stock (see recipe below) or Mushroom Stock (see recipe below)

¼ cup Spanish Aioli (see recipe below)

Salt

Chopped parsley, for garnish

Preheat the oven to 350°F. Remove pasta from its package and, using your hands, break noodles into 1- to 2-inch pieces. Lay the pieces as evenly as possible in a rimmed baking tray, and toast them in the oven until they are an even light brown color. Remove from the oven and set aside to cool.

For the shrimp version of the dish, remove the shells from the shrimp, leaving the tail and head attached. Reserve the shells for the stock. To remove the shrimp vein, run a sharp knife along the back of the shrimp and lift out the vein, then rinse the shrimp carefully and pat dry with a paper towel.

Place a large (16- to 18-inch diameter) paella pan or cast iron skillet over medium-high heat. Season the shrimp with salt, and brown them on one side. Remove the shrimp and set them aside raw-side up until needed.

Add the Onion Sofrito to the pan and cook briefly before pouring in the Shrimp Stock. Increase the heat to high and bring the stock to a boil. Add the toasted pasta. Keep the heat on high until the noodles are tender and the pan is almost dry. At this point, arrange the shrimp, raw-side down, on top of the noodles in the pan. Place rossejat in the oven for about 10 minutes, or until the noodles begin to curl or spike up. Remove the pan from the oven and let it rest a moment. Before serving, drizzle with extra virgin olive oil, and sprinkle with sea salt and chopped parsley. Serve with Spanish Aioli.

For the kielbasa version, slice the sausage into ¼-inch-thick rounds. Place a large (16- to 18-inch diameter) paella pan or cast iron skillet over medium-high heat. Sear sausage pieces on both sides, then set aside until needed.

Add the Onion Sofrito to the pan and cook briefly before pouring in the Mushroom Stock. Increase the heat to high and bring the stock to a boil. Add the toasted pasta. Keep the heat on high until the noodles are tender and the pan is almost dry. At this point, arrange the sausage slices on top of the noodles in the pan. Place rossejat in the oven for about 10 minutes, or until the noodles begin to curl or spike up. Remove the pan from the oven and let it rest a moment. Before serving, drizzle with extra virgin olive oil, and sprinkle with sea salt and chopped parsley. Serve with Spanish Aioli.

## Onion Sofrito

½ cup extra virgin olive oil

2 medium-size Spanish onions, grated

2 garlic cloves, grated

4 large tomatoes, grated

**To make Onion Sofrito:** In a medium-size, heavy-bottomed pot set over very low heat, combine olive oil, onions, and garlic. Cover and cook, stirring occasionally, for 35 to 40 minutes. Add the grated tomatoes and continue cooking until the mixture reaches a paste-like consistency, about 45 more minutes. Remove from heat and let cool, or refrigerate until needed. Extra sauce will keep in the refrigerator for up to 2 weeks.

## Shrimp Stock

Shrimp shells, opened

½ cup vegetable oil

1 medium Spanish onion, cut in large dice

½ pound carrots, peeled and cut in large dice

½ pound celery, trimmed and cut in large dice

2 red bell peppers, stemmed and seeded, cut in large dice

5 garlic cloves, cut in half

3 bay leaves

1 teaspoon freshly ground black pepper

2 teaspoons pimentón de la Vera (Spanish sweet paprika)

3 quarts water

**To make Shrimp Stock:** In a large stockpot, crush the shrimp bodies with a kitchen mallet or a large spoon. Add the oil and roast over medium heat for 3 minutes. Add the onions, carrots, celery, peppers, and garlic. Cook for 5 minutes, then add the bay leaves, black pepper, pimentón de la Vera, and water. Bring to a boil over high heat and reduce to a simmer. Cook uncovered for 45 minutes, then strain the stock through a very fine sieve. Discard the solids. Extra stock can be frozen for up to 6 months.

## Mushroom Stock

2 tablespoons vegetable oil

2 sweet onions, julienned

8 ounces dried mushrooms

5 garlic cloves, smashed

Herb bouquet: 2 sprigs each of thyme, oregano, rosemary

4 quarts water

1 pinch saffron

**To make Mushroom Stock:** In a large stockpot over medium-high heat, heat the oil and add the onions, sweating them until they are translucent. Add the mushrooms, garlic, herbs, and water, and bring to a boil. Reduce heat to medium and cook for 20 minutes. Remove from heat, add the saffron and steep, covered, for 20 minutes. Strain the stock through a very fine sieve. Discard the solids. Extra stock can be frozen for up to six months.

2 large eggs

2 garlic cloves

2 tablespoons freshly squeezed lemon juice

Salt, to taste

½ cup extra virgin olive oil

**To make Aioli:** Place the eggs, garlic, lemon juice, and salt in a blender. Blend on high speed until the mixture comes to a smooth puree. Reduce speed to low and drizzle the oil in a steady stream until it is fully incorporated and the mixture thickens. Transfer to a serving bowl, or refrigerate until needed.

---

## RUSSIAN POTATO SALAD WITH TROUT ROE AND PIQUILLO EMULSION

### (MAKES 4-6 SERVINGS)

3 medium-size potatoes, preferably a waxy variety such as Yukon or Russian Banana

2 medium-size carrots

½ cup sweet peas, blanched and chilled

1 small shallot

2 large eggs

1 cup mayonnaise

Maine sea salt, to taste

Piquillo Emulsion (see recipe below)

Trout roe

Extra virgin olive oil

Place whole potatoes and carrots in a medium-size saucepan and cover with water. Boil over medium-high heat until tender, about 30 minutes. Drain and set aside to cool.

While the vegetables cook, trim the shallot and cut into a very small dice.

Using a clean kitchen towel, peel the potatoes and discard skins. Cut the cooked potatoes and carrots into medium dice and place in a large bowl. Add the diced shallots and blanched sweet peas.

Fill a small pot with about an inch of water and bring to a boil over high heat. Using a large spoon, carefully lower eggs into the pot, cover with a lid, and set a timer for 8 minutes. Reduce heat to medium-high and let the water return to a boil. When the timer is done, drain the pot and fill it with cold water to stop the cooking. When eggs are cool, peel and cut into ½-inch cubes.

Add the eggs to the vegetables, then add mayonnaise and sea salt. Check seasonings, then set aside until ready to serve.

Salad should be served at room temperature. If it is made in advance, refrigerate, but bring to room temperature 30 minutes before serving.

To serve, spread a spoonful of the Piquillo Emulsion on each serving plate and top with potato salad. Spoon a generous amount of trout roe over the salad, then drizzle with olive oil and sprinkle with a small pinch of sea salt.

## Piquillo Emulsion

1 (12-ounce) jar piquillo peppers

2 garlic cloves

1 cup vegetable oil

¼ cup sherry vinegar

Maine sea salt, to taste

**To make Piquillo Emulsion:** In a small, heavy-bottomed pot, combine the peppers, garlic, and oil. Cook over very low heat for 30 minutes, making sure that the mixture doesn't bubble or fry. Remove from heat, drain the oil, and reserve in a separate bowl. Let oil and peppers cool to room temperature.

In the bowl of a food processor or blender, combine the peppers, sherry vinegar, sea salt, and ¼ cup of the reserved oil; puree the ingredients. Continuing to blend, drizzle in the rest of the oil and puree until the mixture is completely emulsified. Check for seasoning, adding more salt, to taste. Leftover sauce will keep in the refrigerator in an airtight container for up to 1 week.

---

# LEMON CURD WITH GRAHAM CRACKERS AND SWISS MERINGUE

### (MAKES 4 SERVINGS)

Lemon Curd (see recipe below)

Swiss Meringue (see recipe below)

Graham Cracker Crumble (see recipe below)

Sweet herbs (such as tangerine lace, mint, basil, bull's blood), for garnish

## Lemon Curd

5 large eggs

5 lemons

6 tablespoons granulated sugar

1 cup (2 sticks) unsalted butter, cut into pieces

Pinch of kosher salt

½ vanilla bean, split

**To make Lemon Curd:** In a medium-size bowl, whisk the eggs. Strain into another bowl and set aside. Zest the lemons with a microplane, then juice them. Set aside zest and juice.

Fill a medium-size pot one-third full with water and place over medium heat. Place a heatproof bowl over the hot water, making a "bain Marie." Add the sugar, lemon zest, lemon juice, butter, salt, and split vanilla bean to the bowl, stirring to combine. When the butter has melted, add the whisked eggs and cook, stirring, until thickened and a thermometer inserted into the mixture reads 170°F. Transfer the curd to a cool bowl, and place a piece of plastic wrap directly on the surface to prevent a skin from forming. Refrigerate curd until chilled, 2 to 3 hours.

## Swiss Meringue

2 egg whites

½ cup granulated sugar

1 pinch cream of tartar

**To make Swiss Meringue:** Fill a medium saucepan one-quarter full of water and bring to a simmer. Combine egg whites, sugar, and cream of tartar in a heatproof bowl, and place over the water. Slowly whisk the mixture over the simmering water until the sugar is dissolved and the whites are warm to the touch but not cooked. Check by touching the whites with your fingers, after 3 to 3½ minutes of cooking; you shouldn't be able to feel any sugar granules. Remove the bowl from the water and, using a handheld electric mixer, whisk, gradually increasing the speed, until stiff peaks form. Place the meringue in a piping bag or bowl and set aside.

### Graham Cracker Crumble

½ cup graham cracker crumbs

2 tablespoons granulated sugar

3 tablespoons unsalted butter

1 pinch of kosher salt

**To make Graham Cracker Crumble:** Preheat oven to 400°F. Line a rimmed baking sheet with parchment paper.

In a small bowl, combine all the ingredients and stir to incorporate. Spread mixture onto the parchment-lined baking sheet. Bake for 10 to 15 minutes, until golden brown and fragrant. Set aside to cool.

**To assemble the dessert:** Spoon the lemon curd into a serving bowl, pipe or spoon a floret of meringue on top and slightly toast it with a culinary blowtorch. Sprinkle crumble over half of the curd and garnish with sweet herbs.

SWEET • SAVORY

## Grab n' Go

# TEN TEN PIÉ

# PASTRIES
— & —
# BENTO LUNCH BOX

DESSERTS • COFFEE
MARKET • BEER • WINE

# Ten Ten Pié

171 Cumberland Avenue
(207) 956-7330
*tentenpieportland.com*
**Restaurant closed in 2019.**
Baker/Owner: Atsuko Fujimoto
Co-Owner: Markos Miller

Opened in 2014 by baker Atsuko Fujimoto and co-owner Markos Miller, Ten Ten Pié (pronounced *pee-ay*) occupies the first floor of a clapboard building in the East End, in a space that for the previous seven decades held the landmark DiPietro's Italian Sandwich Shop. You can still get a sandwich at the current business, but it's more likely to be a Vietnamese Banh Mi, and to come as part of a bento box lunch.

The name Ten Ten Pié comes from Spanish slang for "snack" (Miller was a Spanish teacher before opening the business), and the restaurant's inspirations include classic French baking with fresh local ingredients, Asian convenience stores, and street foods from around the world. In the pastry case, matcha-dusted almond croissants nestle between Finnish *korvapuusti* (a sweet roll with cardamom and quince paste), a popular feta and kale hand pie, and Georgian *khachapuri* topped with golden egg yolk. A rainbow of macarons include chocolate and avocado, and seasonal favorites like caramel apple. At the counter, Maine's largest selection of the Japanese candy Pocky sits next to bags of house-made "pain d'epice" granola.

Baker Atsuko Fujimoto began her career in Tokyo as an editor at a Japanese rock music magazine but moved to Portland with her husband in 2001. In Maine, she switched gears and began working in the pastry kitchen at Fore Street, under the tutelage of renowned Chef Sam Hayward. She had never baked professionally before, and she is still grateful for—and amazed by—the opportunity. Since opening Ten Ten Pié, Fujimoto has become known in her own right, and the restaurant has received local and national acclaim and was included among the best of Portland in *Bon Appetit*'s 2018 feature.

The Pistachio Olive Oil Cake is both gluten-free and dairy-free. At the bakery, ingredients are measured by weight, which has been included in parenthesis.

## PISTACHIO OLIVE OIL CAKE

(MAKES 1 13-INCH LOAF CAKE OR 8 MINI LOAVES OR MUFFIN-SIZE CAKES)

6 large eggs, at room temperature

1 cup (250 grams) granulated sugar, divided

1 cup (240 grams) extra virgin olive oil

2 cups (200 grams) pistachios

1 cup (150 grams) cornmeal

2 tablespoons, plus 2 1/2 teaspoons (30 grams) buckwheat

1 tablespoon lemon zest

Preheat oven to 350°F. Grease a large loaf pan.

In the bowl of a stand mixer fitted with the whisk attachment, combine the eggs and half the sugar. Whip until the mixture is thoroughly incorporated and at the ribbon stage—when the beater is lifted, the mixture will fall back on itself in a thick ribbon. With the mixer on low, slowly pour the olive oil into the egg mixture in a thin stream. Beat until the mixture is completely emulsified and is the consistency of mayonnaise.

Combine remaining sugar, pistachios, cornmeal, buckwheat, and lemon zest in the bowl of a food processor; pulse until the nuts are ground.

Slowly pour the nut mixture into the egg mixture, whisking to incorporate.

Pour the batter into the greased loaf pan and bake for 35 minutes. Rotate pan and bake for an additional 20 minutes, until the center of the cake springs back to the touch.

## COCONUT MILK PANNA COTTA

(MAKES 8 SERVINGS)

3 cups heavy cream

2 cups buttermilk

1 (13.5-ounce) can coconut milk

¾ cup granulated sugar

½ of a vanilla bean

4½ teaspoons powdered gelatin

¼ cup cold water

1 mango

½ cup sugar

½ cup water

Zest and juice of 1 lime

In a medium-size saucepan, combine the cream, buttermilk, coconut milk, sugar, and vanilla bean. Scald over medium heat, stirring to dissolve the sugar.

In a separate small bowl, combine gelatin and water to rehydrate. Strain excess water off the soaked gelatin, then stir into the hot cream mixture. Stir to dissolve gelatin, then strain to remove any clumps. Set the mixture aside to cool.

When the liquid is at room temperature, pour into serving cups and chill for at least 3 hours.

While panna cotta is chilling, cut mango into chunks. In a small saucepan, combine sugar and water and bring to a simmer, stirring to dissolve sugar and creating a simple syrup. Let syrup come to room temperature before tossing with mango, lime zest, and lime juice.

Before serving, top panna cotta with mangos and syrup.

# DESSERTS

COCONUT MILK  4.75
PANNA COTTA

Coffee Gelée  2.95
w/ condensed milk

# DOUGHNUTS

In 1847 Captain Hanson Gregory of Camden, Maine, had an inspiration at sea: The fried cakes and "twisters" he ate aboard his lime trading ship were often crisp on the outer edges but raw and doughy inside. What if he cut a hole in the center to encourage even frying? In his words, quoted from a 1916 interview with the *Washington Post*, "I took the cover off the ship's tin pepper box, and—I cut into the middle of that doughnut the first hole ever seen by mortal eyes!" Behold: the modern doughnut. A Maine tradition ever since, artisan doughnuts made with local potato flour and seasonal fruits have recently exploded in popularity. With sixteen changing flavors offered at two Portland locations, the Holy Donut (194 Park Avenue, and 7 Exchange Street) began the wave in 2012, offering such local favorites as Allen's Coffee Brandy and the addictive Dark Chocolate Sea Salt. More recently, Monument Square's HiFi Donuts (30 City Center) has begun serving a wide array of updated classics, as well as lunch sandwiches on doughnut rolls.

# TERLINGUA

52 Washington Avenue
(207) 808-8502
*terlingua.me*
Pit Master/Owner: Pliny Reynolds
Chef: Wilson Rothschild
Co-Owner: Melanie Reynolds

Opened in 2015, Terlingua was in the vanguard of Washington Avenue's foodie renaissance. Owner and pit master Pliny Reynolds spent a decade living and working as an architect in Austin, Texas, before moving to Maine, and it was in the Lone Star State that he honed his barbecue style. Chef Wilson Rothschild's degree is in cultural anthropology with an emphasis on culinary traditions, and he spent time studying the foods of Central and Southern Mexico. The restaurant's menu combines the two influences, while also leaving room to experiment. Reynolds is just as likely to season a beef brisket with salt and pepper and smoke it over oak as he is to fire up some local lamb ribs with the house Guajillo glaze.

With a pair of longhorns over the poured concrete bar and a large icon of Saint Willie Nelson next to the frozen margarita machine, the feeling at Terlingua is fun and casual. Vintage posters advertising Big Bend National Park and the Rio Grande share wall space with terra cotta tiles, and in summer a few outdoor tables are clustered on the brick sidewalk. From the back, the smell of smoking meat intensifies throughout the day, and patrons are encouraged to come early, as the barbecue specials usually sell out before closing.

At Terlingua, whole peppers are roasted by the bushel in an outdoor drum, but you can roast them under the broiler in the oven at home or over an open flame until the skin blisters and begins to blacken. Once roasted peppers have cooled, their skin should slip off, and they can easily be stemmed and seeded. When working with peppers, be sure to wear gloves if you are seeding by hand. For the recipes below, masa flour, cotija cheese, and Chihuahua cheese are generally available in the Mexican section of your local grocery or online. In a pinch, feta can be substituted for cotija cheese, and Colby or Monterey Jack can replace Chihuahua cheese.

# PORK GREEN CHILI
(MAKES 6-8 SERVINGS)

6 cups diced onions

Canola oil, for sautéing

2 pounds pork butt, diced into ½-inch cubes

1½ ears corn, kernels cut off the cobs

2½ pounds Anaheim peppers, roasted, peeled, seeded, and pureed

¾ pound poblano peppers, roasted, peeled, seeded, and pureed

8 cups water

2 cups tomatoes, diced

2 small potatoes, diced into ¼-inch cubes

2½ tablespoons salt

Masa slurry (¾ cup masa flour mixed with 1 cup water)

Cotija cheese, for serving

In a large, heavy-bottomed pot, sweat onions on low heat for 30 minutes, until soft and translucent. Add pork, corn, pureed peppers, and water and simmer for 1½ hours, or until pork is tender. Add tomatoes, potatoes, and salt, to taste. Stir in masa slurry by tablespoons, thickening to desired consistency. Serve immediately, garnished with crumbled cotija cheese.

# ENCHILADAS SUIZAS (POTATO ENCHILADAS)
### (SERVES 8 SERVINGS)

Filling (see recipe below)

Sauce (see recipe below)

16 corn tortillas

Canola oil, for frying

Avocado slices, for serving

Chopped cilantro, for serving

Cotija cheese, grated, for serving

Pico de gallo salsa, for serving

## Filling

5 pounds potatoes

1 tablespoon salt

6 ears corn, shucked

2½ pounds shredded Chihuahua cheese

1 cup sliced scallions

Salt and freshly ground pepper, to taste

## Filling

To make the filling: Peel potatoes and dice into ½-inch cubes. Place potatoes in a large, heavy-bottomed pot and cover with water. Add salt and bring potatoes to a simmer over medium-high heat, cooking until tender. Drain potatoes in a colander and set aside to cool.

Heat a gas or charcoal grill. Place the ears of corn on the grill, cooking until kernels are tender and some have grill marks. Cool corn and cut kernels from the cob.

In a large bowl, combine potatoes, corn, shredded cheese, and sliced scallions. Taste for seasoning, adding salt and freshly ground pepper as desired.

## Sauce

2 pounds tomatillos, husks removed

1 medium onion, sliced

6 cloves garlic

6 jalapeños

1 bunch cilantro

2 tablespoons kosher salt

2 cups roasted poblano peppers, peeled and seeded

3 cups sour cream

To make the sauce: Preheat oven to 400°F. Place tomatillos, onion, garlic, and jalapeños on a rimmed baking sheet and roast for 10 minutes, until vegetables begin to soften. Remove from oven and cool.

Place roasted vegetables, cilantro, salt, and roasted poblanos in the bowl of a food processor; blend until smooth. Pour sauce into a pot and add water to bring to desired consistency. Stir in sour cream.

## Enchiladas

To assemble the enchiladas: In a flat-bottomed skillet, fry corn tortillas in a small amount of canola oil for 3 seconds on each side. Remove to a plate to cool. Place 3 tablespoons of filling on each tortilla and roll tightly. Before serving, place ¼ cup of sauce in a skillet and heat rolled enchilada in the sauce for 3 to 4 minutes. To serve, place enchiladas and the sauce they were cooked in on a plate and top with sliced avocado, grated cotija cheese, chopped cilantro, and pico de gallo salsa.

# THE SHOP AT ISLAND CREEK OYSTERS

123 Washington Avenue
(207) 699-4466
*portland.islandcreekoysters.com*
General Manager: Kit Paschal

This northern outpost of Duxbury, Massachusetts' Island Creek Oysters boasts a carefully curated selection of shellfish sourced from the waters of Maine and New England in its raw bar, as well as caviars and imported tinned fish and *conservas* from Spain. In an old brick building on Washington Avenue's foodiest stretch, The Shop is a combination wholesale business and retail raw bar and market, and it was featured in *Bon Appetit*'s 2018 roundup of the best of Portland. Knowledgeable staff shuck oysters, pair them with local and imported wines and beers, and deliver them by the dozen to communal tables and wicker love seats arranged inside the shop and on a relaxed seasonal patio. In the market, seafood, shucking tools, and a smattering of books on oysters and sustainable aquaculture can be bought for home.

Bottarga, a firm block of salt cured of tuna roe, is a Mediterranean delicacy that adds a briny, slightly bitter bite to the compound butter below. A favorite among chefs, bottarga can be purchased at specialty shops or online. A little goes a long way, and it's generally used sparingly, shaved with a microplane and sprinkled on or incorporated into dishes. Preserved lemon is a pungent Middle Eastern condiment that can also be found at specialty shops and online.

# CHAMPAGNE MIGNONETTE

(MAKES 1 SERVING)

1 cup Champagne vinegar

½ cup sparkling wine (prosecco or Champagne are best)

1 cup finely minced shallots

Freshly ground black pepper, to finish

Combine all ingredients except pepper and stir to integrate. Add a few turns of freshly ground pepper right before serving.

# GRILLED OYSTERS WITH HERBED BOTTARGA BUTTER AND PRESERVED LEMON

(MAKES 4 SERVINGS)

12 medium to large Maine oysters

Compound butter (see recipe below)

Chives, snipped

### Compound Butter

1 pound unsalted butter at room temperature

⅓ ounce (10 grams) piece bottarga (salt-cured tuna roe)

½ preserved lemon

2 tablespoons whole milk

1 tablespoon flat-leaf parsley, roughly chopped

Sea salt, to taste

**To prepare Compound Butter:** Using a microplane, shave the bottarga. Remove the flesh from the preserved lemon, and finely chop the lemon peel.

Combine butter, bottarga, and preserved lemon peel in a mixing bowl; use a hand mixer on low to mix the ingredients. After 2 minutes, slowly increase mixer speed while adding milk. Whip on high for another 3 to 4 minutes. Add parsley during the last 2 minutes. Taste, and adjust seasoning, adding sea salt if desired.

**To cook the oysters:** Heat a grill until it is medium hot. Shuck oysters, detaching the abductor muscle from the bottom shell.

Place oysters directly on grill or grill pan. Be careful not to spill too much of the natural liquor. Add a dollop of compound butter to each oyster.

Let cook until oyster and butter are both bubbling. The goal is to be warmed through but not overcooked and rubbery. Garnish with a small pinch of chives.

# OYSTERS

Mollusks, crustaceans, and all kinds of fish thrive in the cold waters off the rocky coast of Maine, and all along the coast, conditions are ideal for the cultivation of oysters. From the crisp, meaty Little Bays harvested near Eliot in the south, to the dense, briny Glidden Points found in the deep waters at the mouth of the midcoast Damariscotta River and the deep cupped, metallic Taunton Bays found near northern Acadia Park, oysters' characters are shaped by the waters in which they've grown. Though some oysters are exported beyond state lines, the majority are from small producers who harvest just enough to tantalize gourmands around Maine. For a guided tasting of the season's best, stop by one of Portland's many raw bars, from the casual Shop at Island Creek Oysters (page 183) to the elegant Scales (page 161), which juts out on a pier overlooking the working waterfront.

6" serves 6-8

9" serves 10-16

1/4 sheet serves 16-24

12" serves 24-36

1/2 sheet serves 36-52

Cake Sizes

## CAKE FLAVORS

Boston Cream

Chocolate

Lemon

Orange

Red Velvet

• Yellow (Vanilla)

## FROSTING FLAVORS

Almond

Chocolate

Cream Cheese

Lemon

Mocha

Orange

Peanut Butter

Raspberry

Strawberry

• Vanilla

## PIES

9" $18

apple • blueberry • butterscotch cream •
cherry • chocolate cream •
lemon meringue • mixed berry •
peach • peanut butter •
pecan • pumpkin •
raspberry •
strawberry-
rhubarb

made-to-order

THE LANGUAGE ARCHIVE
BY JULIA CHO

DIRECTED BY
CHRISTOPHER PRICE

SEPTEMBER 20 - OCTOBER 7, 2018
Thurs - Sat at 7:30
Sundays at 2:00

Tickets: MADHORSE.COM
or call 767 - 0848

Mad Horse Theatre
24 Mosher Street
South Portland, ME

# TIN PAN BAKERY

**897 Brighton Avenue**
**(207) 310-4405**
*tinpanbakery.com*
Baker/Owner Elise Richer

Tucked along an unassuming stretch of Brighton Avenue, Tin Pan Bakery stands out for its unpretentious, warmly modern aesthetic—accented by an ever-expanding collection of vintage tin baking pans—and its bright cases filled with freshly made pastries. The menu in this classic neighborhood bakery is contemporary American, with nods to owner/baker Elise Richer's Jewish and Norwegian heritage. Cardamom pound cake and chocolate babka mingle with classic fruit-filled bar cookies, brownies and blondies, and sweetly iced vanilla, chocolate, and red velvet cupcakes. Savory hand pies, fluffy cheddar biscuits, and potato and kasha knishes round out the homey offerings, chalked daily onto the wall.

Richer came to baking after years of policy work in Washington, D.C., and honed her skills at D.C.'s famed CakeLove bakery. Returning to her native New England in 2004, she began a home-based wholesale baking business and published a cookbook, *Always in Season*, before opening the shop in 2017.

The bars below can be made with either fresh or frozen blueberries, but try to make them Maine grown! Maine blueberries are small but mighty, packed with flavor and the perfect balance of sweet and tart. At the bakery the pan is cut into twelve generous bars, but at home feel free to cut them smaller.

The crumb cake can also be made with fresh or frozen fruit. If rhubarb is unavailable, berries make a lovely alternative.

# BLUEBERRY CORNMEAL BARS

## (MAKES 12 GENEROUS BARS)

1 cup plus 6 tablespoons (2¾ sticks) unsalted butter

1 teaspoon lemon zest

1 teaspoon pure vanilla extract

2 cups sugar, divided

2½ cups flour

1⅓ cups cornmeal

1¾ teaspoons baking powder

1 teaspoon salt

½ teaspoon ground ginger

3 cups blueberries

2 tablespoons cornstarch

1 tablespoon lemon juice

Preheat oven to 350°F. Grease a 9 x 13-inch pan.

In a small saucepan over low heat, melt the butter. Remove from heat and stir in the lemon zest and vanilla extract and set aside.

In a large bowl, combine 1½ cups sugar, flour, cornmeal, baking powder, salt, and ground ginger; whisk together until thoroughly combined. Pour in the melted butter mixture and mix with a wooden spoon until no dry spots remain. Measure 1 cup of this mixture, place in a bowl, and set aside.

Press the remainder of the mixture into the prepared pan, pressing the dough firmly into the corners. Bake for 20 minutes, until golden brown. Remove from oven and increase oven temperature to 375°F.

While the base is baking, prepare the blueberries. In a medium-size bowl, toss berries with remaining ½ cup of sugar, cornstarch, and lemon juice.

When the base is completely baked, pour the blueberry mixture over it and use a spatula to spread berries across the entire surface. Take the reserved cup of cornmeal mixture and crumble it across the top of the berries, scattering the clumps as evenly as possible.

Bake 25 to 30 minutes, until top is lightly browned and the berries look slightly dried. Let the bars cool before cutting. Chill before serving, as the bars become soft and crumbly if left at room temperature.

# RHUBARB CRUMB CAKE

## (MAKES ONE 9 x 13-INCH CAKE)

1½ pounds rhubarb, sliced ½- to ¾-inch thick (roughly 6 cups)

⅓ cup sugar

2¼ cups flour

2 tablespoons potato starch (or cornstarch)

1 cup, plus 2 tablespoons sugar

½ teaspoon salt

½ teaspoon baking soda

½ teaspoon baking powder

¼ teaspoon cardamom

½ teaspoon cinnamon

¾ cup (1½ sticks) unsalted butter

⅔ cup buttermilk

3 eggs

1 teaspoon pure vanilla extract

Crumb Topping (see recipe below)

Preheat oven to 325°F. Grease a 9 x 13-inch pan. Place rhubarb in a bowl with sugar and toss to combine. Set aside.

Place flour, potato starch (or cornstarch), sugar, salt, baking soda, baking powder, cardamom, and cinnamon in the bowl of a stand mixer fitted with the paddle attachment. Turn the mixer on low and beat a few times to blend the dry ingredients. Cut butter into pieces and add to the mixture, continuing to beat on low speed for 1 to 2 minutes to incorporate. The mixture should be the consistency of wet sand, with no visible lumps of butter. Make sure not to overbeat.

In a measuring cup or separate bowl, combine buttermilk, eggs, and vanilla. Whisk until fully blended.

Turn the mixer back on low speed and pour in the wet ingredients. After a minute, increase mixer speed to medium high and mix for an additional 15 seconds. The batter should be fully blended and smooth. Scrape down the sides if necessary to incorporate all of the mixture.

Spread the batter into the prepared pan. Using a slotted spoon, remove the rhubarb from its bowl (leaving behind any exuded juices) and scatter slices over the top. Sprinkle the crumb topping over the top of the cake.

Bake for 30 minutes, then check for doneness. A toothpick or cake tester inserted into the middle of the cake should come out clean. If cake needs more time, return to oven, lowering the heat to 300°F to avoid overbrowning the edges. Serve cake warm or at room temperature.

## Crumb Topping

7 tablespoons unsalted butter, softened

⅔ cup flour

⅓ cup light brown sugar

¼ cup sugar

⅛ teaspoon salt

½ teaspoon cinnamon

To make the crumb topping: In a medium-size bowl, combine all ingredients. Using your fingers, mix together, making crumbs about the size of dried beans. Set aside.

# BLUEBERRIES

Tiny, juicy, and intensely flavorful, wild blueberries are one of Maine's most delectable summer treats. Their scrubby plants dot roadsides around the state, marked by soft green foliage and clumps of white, bell-shaped flowers in June that become dark, sweet berries by the August harvest, then turn the color of flame as the fall progresses. North of Bar Harbor, along the Downeast coast, more than 60,000 acres of wild blueberries grow in fields and barrens, where they're managed and harvested by farmers, who export this delicacy around the country. In the rest of the state, Mainers still go picking in the manner immortalized by Robert McCloskey in his classic children's book *Blueberries for Sal*, fanning out with pails over reliable hills and bringing quarts of berries home to make jams and pies. Look for blueberries in season at markets and roadside stands, and any time of year frozen, dried, and in preserves.

# TIPO

182 Ocean Avenue
207-358-7970
*tiporestaurant.com*
Chef/Owner: Chris Gould
Co-Owner: Paige Gould

Set away from the peninsula in Portland's residential Back Cove neighborhood, Tipo is a casual, family-oriented spot with a changing menu of Italian-inspired pizzas, pastas, and plates. The second restaurant from Chef Chris and Paige Gould, of the Old Port's Central Provisions (page 33), Tipo embraces family dining, while keeping the menu in line with the couple's commitment to inventive flavors and local ingredients. The wide range of offerings feature flavorful homemade pastas with rich, meaty sauces; small plates of seasonal vegetables, antipasti, house-made mozzarella and goat sausage; and pizzas made in the central brick oven, visible from most tables. Occasionally, Tipo hosts a "Guest Chef" pizza series, inviting chefs from other restaurants to make pies for a night. A few evenings a week, the bar—cheerfully covered with license plates from across the country—offers a happy hour, with a special menu of Italian wines and cocktails, and snacks that go a step beyond: chicharrones with hot sauce, fennel pollen and lime, and nduja crostini with pesto, golden raisins, and radish greens.

Both pillowy and chewy, topped with sweet onion and pungent rosemary, the Caramelized Onion Focaccia below is one of Tipo's most popular menu items. Made with a wet dough, focaccia spreads and makes a large, flat loaf. Chef Gould measures by weight, which is included in parenthesis. As with any yeast bread, keep timing in mind, and make sure to give yourself plenty of time for the dough to rise.

At Tipo, the Pork Ragu with Oregano and Mascarpone is served with a housemade rye cavatelli, but for home, substitute fresh or dry cavatelli or rigatoni.

# SPICY PORK RAGU WITH OREGANO AND MASCARPONE
### (MAKES 8 SERVINGS)

| | |
|---|---|
| 1 teaspoon black pepper | ½ cup white wine |
| 1 teaspoon coriander | 1 tablespoon salt |
| 1 teaspoon fennel seeds | 1 tablespoon soy sauce |
| 5 sprigs fresh thyme | 1 teaspoon fish sauce |
| 1 bay leaf | 1 teaspoon chardonnay vinegar |
| 2–3 tablespoons canola oil | 1 tablespoon Agrumato lemon olive oil (see note) |
| 2 pounds ground pork | Salt, to taste |
| 1 Spanish onion, minced | 1 pound cavatelli or rigatoni |
| 1 small carrot, scraped and minced | ⅓ cup mascarpone |
| 1 red bell pepper, stemmed, seeded, and minced | 2 tablespoons fresh oregano, chopped |
| 4 cloves garlic, minced | ⅓ cup pecorino romano, freshly grated |

Note: If you can't find Agrumato lemon olive oil, you can substitute a flavorful finishing olive oil combined with 1 teaspoon lemon zest.

Assemble a sachet of herbs, placing pepper, coriander, fennel seeds, thyme, and bay leaf in a square of cheesecloth. Gather the sides and tie together with butchers' twine. You will have a little "purse" of spices and herbs. Set aside until ready to use.

Place a large, heavy-bottomed pot over medium-high heat, adding just enough canola oil to coat the bottom. Add the ground pork and cook until browned, 7–10 minutes. Remove the meat and set aside in a bowl.

Add the onion, carrot, and bell pepper to the pot, cooking until soft, 5–7 minutes. Add the garlic and cook until fragrant, 2–3 minutes. Deglaze the pan by pouring in the wine and scraping the bottom with a wooden spoon until all of the brown bits that might be left behind have been dissolved. Return the meat to the pot with the vegetables. Add the salt and the sachet and cook over low heat at a simmer for 2 hours, until the sauce is reduced and the meat is tender. Season with soy sauce, fish sauce, vinegar, Agrumato, and salt.

To serve: Bring a large pot of salted water to the boil and cook pasta according to package directions until al dente. In a separate large pot, combine drained pasta with the warm ragu and mascarpone, cooking the mixture over medium-low heat for a few minutes to let the flavors meld together. Serve garnished with fresh oregano and grated pecorino.

# CARAMELIZED ONION FOCACCIA

(MAKES ONE LARGE TRAY LOAF)

2½ cups (620g) water, at 72 degrees

4 tablespoons plus 2 1/2 teaspoons (40g) active yeast

1 teaspoon (4g) sugar

7 cups (1000g) 00 pizza flour

5 teaspoons (25g) salt

½ cup (125g) rosemary-infused olive oil

4 tablespoons chopped Calabrian chili

⅓ cup caramelized onions (see note)

⅓ cup chopped rosemary

Maldon sea salt

Red onions, sliced and tossed with mixture of ½ canola oil and ½ rosemary-infused olive oil

Note: To caramelize the onions, cook sliced yellow onions in olive oil, cooking over medium heat until richly fragrant and golden, about 30 minutes.

In the bowl of a stand mixer fitted with the dough hook, combine water, yeast, and sugar, and let stand for 10 minutes, until the yeast is creamy. Add flour, salt, olive oil, chili, and caramelized onions and mix on speed 2 for 3 minutes. Cover with a clean kitchen towel and let rise for 1 hour, until dough is doubled in size.

Remove dough from bowl, flatten to shape on the tray, and rub with olive oil. Let dough rest 5 minutes.

Evenly prick the dough with a skewer, making sure that there are no large bubbles trapped in the dough. Garnish with rosemary, sea salt, and red onion slices, and wrap loosely with plastic wrap. Let rise for 45 minutes.

While dough is rising, preheat oven to 425. Bake for 10 minutes, then turn tray and bake for an additional 7 minutes. When fully baked, remove from oven and cool on a rack before serving.

# UNION

Press Hotel
390 Congress Street
(207) 808-8700
*unionportland.com*
Chef: Josh Berry

Situated on the first floor of the Press Hotel, in a building formerly occupied by the offices of the *Portland Press Herald*, Union offers dishes of what Chef Josh Berry likes to call "enhanced local cuisine." Compressed melon, popcorn dust, and bright, house-made emulsions and sauces accent a menu that combines beautifully prepared local favorites with palate-expanding specials. Chef Berry, a Maine native, has returned to the state after honing his skills in restaurants in Europe and New England, most recently serving as the executive chef at the acclaimed Stowe Mountain Lodge in Vermont. His enthusiasm for the flavors of home is evident in the deep Maine roots of the menu—locally foraged elderberries, knobby heirloom apples, and honey from hives kept on the roof of the hotel are woven into the offerings, as are a wide range of local seafood, meats, and poultry. The space is both gracious and comfortable, with an open kitchen in full view of all seating and a wall mounted with antique typewriters, in a nod to the building's history.

Fresh lobster is the key to Union's acclaimed lobster rolls. If you're pressed for time, some fish markets can boil the lobster for you, and some will even pick the meat. The most important thing is that it's fresh and sweet—never use frozen lobster in a roll. When choosing fish for the Pan-Seared Cod, look for the thickest, firmest part of the fillet. Once it is cooked through, it will flake delicately, one of cod's best features. Dredging in instant flour like Wondra will crisp the edges of each piece without overwhelming them.

# MAINE LOBSTER ROLL WITH LEMON MAYONNAISE

(MAKES 4 "LOBSTAH" ROLLS)

2 1½-pound live Maine lobsters

½ cup Lemon Mayonnaise (see recipe below)

4 tablespoons unsalted butter,
   divided and softened

4 New England–style top-split rolls

4 teaspoons snipped chives

Bring a large pot of salted water to the boil. Place lobsters in the pot and return to the boil. Cook lobsters for 12–14 minutes, until they are bright scarlet. Using tongs and being careful not to scald your hands, remove the cooked lobsters from the hot water and place in ice water to chill. When lobsters are cool enough to handle, remove the meat. Chop the tail and claw meat into bite-size pieces, using the knuckle meat as a guide for size. Toss the lobster with the mayonnaise, and set aside.

Spread the softened butter on each side of the rolls, and cook on a griddle or skillet until golden brown. Divide the lobster salad between the rolls, and top with the snipped chives before serving.

## Lemon Mayonnaise

1 large egg

1 teaspoon Dijon mustard

½ teaspoon kosher salt

1 tablespoon white vinegar

2 tablespoons freshly squeezed lemon juice

Dash smoked paprika

1 cup canola oil

Place egg in blender, and add mustard, salt, vinegar, lemon juice, paprika, and ¼ cup of the oil. Turn on the blender, and while it is running, slowly add the remaining oil in a thin stream. Blend mixture until it is the desired consistency.

## PAN-SEARED COD WITH LITTLENECK CLAMS, BOK CHOY, AND CHINESE FERMENTED CABBAGE

### (MAKES 4 SERVINGS)

2 tablespoons canola oil

8 3-ounce portions of cod, cut from the thickest part of the fillet

Salt and freshly ground black pepper

¼ cup instant flour (such as Wondra)

6 tablespoons unsalted butter, chilled and cut into small pieces

2 shallots, trimmed and sliced

2 tablespoons minced garlic

½ cup thinly sliced Chinese fermented sausage

6 heads baby bok choy, cleaned and halved

16 littleneck clams, scrubbed, rinsed and patted dry

¼ cup soy sauce

1 cup water

Juice of one lemon

Chopped cilantro, for serving

Preheat oven to 350°F.

Heat a large, heavy-bottomed skillet over medium heat, then add the canola oil and swirl pan to evenly coat the surface. Pat dry the cod, and season with salt and pepper. Dust the fish with instant flour. Gently place the fish in the hot pan. Drop in the butter and swirl it around the fish until the butter is browned. Flip the cod once the bottom is golden brown, and cook for an additional 1–2 minutes. Remove fish from the pan and place on a baking tray. Place in the oven for 7–10 minutes, until the cod is just cooked through.

While the fish is in the oven, add the shallots, garlic, Chinese sausage, bok choy, and clams to the pan of brown butter. Stir the ingredients until they "get to know each other." Add the soy sauce and water to the pan to deglaze it and bring up the bits that have stuck to the bottom. Cover the pan and cook until the clams are open. Taste the broth, adjusting the seasoning if needed.

To serve, divide the ingredients in the pan between four bowls. Top with two pieces of the seared cod, and garnish with a dash of lemon juice and chopped cilantro.

# WOODFORD FOOD & Beverage

660 Forest Avenue
(207) 200-8503
*woodfordfb.com*
Co-Owners: Birch Shambaugh and Fayth Preyer
Chef: Courtney Loreg

In an iconic pitched-roofed building that was once a Valle's Steakhouse, Woodford Food & Beverage straddles many roles, at the intersection of several neighborhoods. With a brasserie vibe that channels the 1950s, the restaurant functions as both a neighborhood bar and a destination dining room, with intimate booths, a mirror-backed bar, and decor that includes a coveted few old-fashioned glasses from the original Valle's and a curated collection of vinyl. Married co-owners Birch Shambaugh and Fayth Preyer, and Chef Courtney Loreg, came up in some of the best kitchens in Portland and New York City, and their backgrounds are showcased in the contemporary, regionally infused fare that pairs French bistro and American classics: oysters, *moules frites*, and *croque monsieur* share the menu with deviled eggs, a brisket hamburger, Maine crab cakes, and colossal shrimp cocktail. It's a place for date nights, but also for families, with a kids' menu full of slightly adventurous meals and fun culinary puzzles and riddles. (Why do the French like to eat snails? Because they don't like fast food!)

　　Much like the restaurant itself, the recipes featured here bring an updated local twist to the classics. Made with rose hip syrup—at the Woodford's bar, the rose hips are foraged from a nearby beach—the Negroni Rugosa is a seaside riff meant to showcase the elemental beauty of the Maine coast. Available only in late summer, the fried green tomatoes remind diners of the seasonality of New England, while the pick-led cucumbers and chow chow preserve a taste of the summer bounty. Fried green tomatoes can be made in any quantity, and the proportions may change slightly depending on the juiciness of the tomatoes. The aim is for a crisp crust surrounding tender tomato, served piping hot.

## NEGRONI RUGOSA
(MAKES 1 GENEROUS COCKTAIL)

1 ounce Plymouth gin

.75 ounce Campari

.75 ounce Rose Hip Syrup (see recipe below)

.75 ounce Dolin blanc vermouth

.5 ounce dry rosé

Orange peel, for garnish

Combine all ingredients in a cocktail shaker with cracked ice. Shake well and strain into an old-fashioned glass with ice cubes. Garnish with orange peel.

Rose Hip Syrup

4 cups rose hips

2 cups water

1 cup sugar

To make Rose Hip Syrup: Thoroughly wash rose hips, being sure to remove stems and any remnants of the flowers. In a medium-size nonreactive saucepan, bring rose hips and water to a simmer and cook, covered, for 15 minutes. Let mixture cool slightly and strain through a jelly bag or a cheesecloth-lined chinois. If any particles remain, strain a second time. Return clear rose hip juice to the saucepan, stir in sugar, and return to a simmer for another 5 minutes, stirring regularly. Cool syrup and refrigerate in an airtight container for up to 2 weeks.

# PICKLED GINGER CUCUMBERS

### (MAKES 1 QUART)

1 large piece ginger root

2 large cucumbers, sliced into ½-inch rounds

2 cups white wine vinegar

4 cups water

½ cup salt

½ cup sugar

1 bay leaf

1 star anise

3 tablespoons coriander seeds

1 teaspoon chile flakes

3 tablespoons mustard seeds

Preheat oven to 350°F. Cut ginger root into three or four chunks and roast until pieces begin to shrivel and become aromatic, about 30 minutes.

Pack sliced cucumbers into two glass pint jars, leaving enough room to cover with pickling liquid.

Combine remaining ingredients in a large pot and bring to a boil. Add roasted ginger. Pour hot liquid over cucumbers and allow to stand until cooled to room temperature. Cover and store in the refrigerator. Pickles will keep, refrigerated, for up to 2 weeks.

# FRIED GREEN TOMATO WITH CREAMY ROASTED GARLIC HERB SAUCE AND VEGETABLE CHOW CHOW

(MAKES 8 SERVINGS)

Creamy Roasted Garlic Herb Sauce (see recipe below)

Vegetable Chow Chow (see recipe below)

Fried Green Tomatoes (see recipe below)

## Creamy Roasted Garlic Herb Sauce

1 cup sour cream

1 cup mayonnaise

1½ teaspoons dried oregano

½ teaspoon freshly ground black pepper

½ teaspoon paprika

2–3 dashes hot sauce (such as Tabasco)

2–3 garlic cloves, roasted and smashed

½–1 cup buttermilk

Salt, to taste

**To make Creamy Roasted Garlic Herb Sauce:** In a medium-size mixing bowl, combine all ingredients except buttermilk, whisking until smooth. Add ½ cup buttermilk, stirring until thoroughly combined. If thinner sauce is desired, add up to ½ cup more buttermilk. Salt to taste, and refrigerate until serving.

## Vegetable Chow Chow

2 ears corn, kernels cut from cob

1 large green tomato, cut into small dice

1 large sweet onion, cut into small dice

1 medium zucchini, cut into small dice

Brine (see recipe below)

**To make Vegetable Chow Chow:** In a medium-size bowl, place all the vegetables, tossing to combine. Spoon mixture into pint glass jars, leaving space for brine.

Pour hot brine over the mixed vegetables and allow to stand until cooled to room temperature. Cover with jar lids and store in refrigerator for up to a month.

## Brine

3 cups apple cider vinegar

6 cups water

¼ cup salt

1 tablespoon ground cumin

1 tablespoon ground coriander

2 tablespoons paprika

2 tablespoons ground turmeric

1 raw garlic clove

**To make Brine:** In a large pot, combine all the ingredients and bring to a boil.

## Fried Green Tomatoes

4 green tomatoes, sliced into ¼-inch-thick rounds

1½ teaspoons kosher salt

1 cup flour

2 eggs

1 cup panko

Canola oil, for frying

**To make Fried Green Tomatoes:** Salt each round of tomato and dredge in flour. Dip in egg and then coat with panko. Fry in a cast iron skillet or a deep fryer until crisp and golden.

**To serve the dish:** Serve the Fried Green Tomatoes hot, with Creamy Roasted Garlic Herb Sauce and a garnish of Chow Chow.

# STEAK

## COCKTAILS

*happy hour*

# SEAFOOD

## BRUNCH

# GOOD TIMES

# FOODIE TOURS

With so many wonderful restaurants, it's hard to know where to begin. Enter the foodie tour. As Portland's culinary scene has grown, several businesses have begun offering curated samplings of the city, helping steer visitors to the city's best offerings and a few hidden gems. Maine Foodie Tours (mainefoodietours.com) provides guided walking tours year-round, with experiences that range from an overview of Portland's classics to themed tours that focus on specific areas of interest. Maine Food for Thought Tours (mainefoodforthought.com) explore "the story behind the plate," with a "Land, Sea to Fork Tour" that offers a behind-the-scenes look—and taste—at six nationally acclaimed restaurants.

# Acknowledgments

Just as Portland's food scene is a collaborative endeavor, this book has been the work of many. The greatest thanks go to the incredible chefs and restaurateurs who make Portland their home. Your generosity in sharing stories and recipes, and in making time for Karl to photograph your faces, kitchens, and beautifully plated dishes, has been astounding. We feel honored to know you and eat your food, and humbled to attempt its re-creation in our own kitchen.

Special thanks go to our dear friend Leslie Oster, without whose guidance and many introductions this book wouldn't have been possible. Thanks also to the Portland Food Map and the great food writers of Maine, who never steer us astray.

For help testing and scaling recipes, special thanks go to Elyse, Lauren, Monika and David Eichler, Anna and Julie Greene, Anya and Zach Heiden, and the K-5th grade aftercare student chefs at Levey Day School. Thanks also to our friends who served as taste testers as we cooked our way through the manuscript—Thanksgiving guests, we're looking at you.

Thanks to my supremely patient editor, Michael Steere, for suggesting the project and giving us an excuse to hire a sitter and go out to dinner—all in the name of research. Thanks to the whole production team behind the book, particularly Karen Ackermann. Thanks also to my agents, Cheryl Pientka and Katelyn Detweiler at Jill Grinberg Literary Management, for their guidance, diligence, and steady support.

Thanks to our children, Charlotte, Beatrice, and Sadie, for their patience as we juggled everyone's schedules and tried to keep our lives organized. We are blessed by your expansive palates and forgiving natures.

Finally, thanks to the amazing farmers, foragers, and fisherpeople of Maine. Without you, we would have no food to write about.

# ABOUT THE AUTHOR and PHOTOGRAPHER

Margaret Hathaway is the author *The Year of the Goat, Living with Goats,* the *Food Lovers' Guide to Maine*, and the first *Portland, Maine Chef's Table* cookbook. Photographer Karl Schatz is the principal of MaineMessage. The couple lives with their three children on Ten Apple Farm, their homestead in southern Maine, where they raise dairy goats and assorted livestock and poultry, tend a large garden and small orchard, make cheese, and lead goat hikes though their woods. Visit them at TenAppleFarm.com.

# INDEX OF RECIPES BY CATEGORY